CRITICAL PARANOIA

NCQ TITLES

Legal Fictions
Politics & Letters
On Yeats: Upon a House
Drama & Democracy
Locating Theology

Time Pieces
Critical Paranoia
On Joyce: 3 easy essays
On Eliot
Literary Conversions

Film texts

A Trip to Rome
A Short Break in Budapest
the Last Priest of Horus
WWW: the weekend that warped the world

A Week in Venice
Four Days in Athens
Magic in Prague

Play texts
Darwin: an evolutionary entertainment
Strange Meetings & Shorts

Eliotics

Forthcoming
Rubbishing Hockney & other reviews
On Collecting Walter Benjamin
Autobiography & Class Consciousness
Considering Canterbury Cathedral

*Though each can be read independently,
these NCQ publications, taken together,
comprise a single hyper-text collection*

CRITICAL PARANOIA

Bernard Sharratt

New Crisis Quarterly
2015

NEW CRISIS QUARTERLY

ncq@newcrisisquarterly.myzen.co.uk

First published 2015

ISBN : 978-1-910956-08-3

For
Venkat and Shobha Rao
for much else besides
generous hospitality
in Hyderabad

CONTENTS

Acknowledgements

'Critical paranoia': published in *The Literary Labyrinth*, 1984.

'Literary value?' : published in *Reading Relations*, 1982.

'Enclaves & Cul-de-sacs': a version appeared in *New Blackfriars*, February 1978.

'Cybertheory' : published in *The State of Theory*, edited by Richard Bradford, Routledge, 1993.

'Communications & Image Studies': a version appeared in *Comparative Criticism 11: The Future of the Disciplines,* edited by E.S.Shaffer, CUP, 1989. Reprinted with permission from Cambridge University Press.

'Teaching & Multimedia in India': a version was published in *Humanities and Pedagogy*, edited by K.C. Baral, Delhi, 2002.

FOREWORD

The first piece in this short compilation of fairly loosely linked essays was published in 1984, in my *The Literary Labyrinth*, which consisted mainly of reviews of imaginary books I didn't have the time actually to write, including the fictive book which gives this volume its title. The penultimate piece offers two versions of a leaflet publicising a multi-disciplinary degree programme which lasted from 1986 to 2000 and was the first UK Humanities degree to incorporate in practice and to critique in theoretical analysis the then rapidly developing innovations in interactive digital multimedia, in hyper-text composition, and what was to become the internet. In particular, we were intrigued by the proliferation of new forms and functions of 'images'—hence the overall title of the degree: 'Communications & Image Studies'.

That pioneering programme, nicknamed 'CIS', is also now only to be imagined, since it was dis-continued by a Vice-Chancellor who maintained in the late 1990s that any academic programme making extensive use of computers should be located only under the aegis of Business Studies, and by a University Research Assessment Exercise which could only classify what we were doing as 'Library Science'. Such, such were the days.

Between these two pieces I have assembled some traces from moments in that transition, in my own case and far more generally, from the concerns of a traditional 'literary criticism', through the influences of several competing and converging theoretical positions and problems, to engagement with the various digital developments which have so considerably re-shaped the last few decades. Readers who have no particular interest in traversing discarded theoretical terrains might perhaps begin at, say, 'Cybertheory', and I apologise if they have already paid for a few dozen skipped pages—though it is sometimes the hardest of historical tasks to comprehend those moments which immediately preceded one's own current concerns.

It was actually considerable fun to ride those waves, especially the early excitements of the digital revolution, and it may be worth recording some aspects of them before they fade from memory entirely, if only because the relevance and validity of some at least of those concerns and approaches may once again be recognised as not wholly surpassed or superceded, as yet another 'new crisis' engulfs us.

This short book might be read in conjunction with a collection of some of the reviews responding to the digital developments of that period which I was lucky enough to publish in the *New York Times*, assembled in a volume probably to be entitled *Rubbishing Hockney*. More work from that period might also appear in other NCQ books.

The title of my imprint *New Crisis Quarterly* revives that of an exceedingly short-lived periodical: its first, only, and farewell issue appeared in 1984—under the guise of *The Literary Labyrinth*, the readers of which were invited, if so inclined, to write the reviewed but imaginary books themselves. That overall invitation to readers remains the same, to complete a work if they so wish: that of a moment in which the genuine critical and political potential of the new digital developments had not yet been almost completely stifled by the purely commercial priorities which now dominate the digital terrain. Perhaps we should have transferred to Business Studies after all.

My debt to various colleagues from that trajectory is substantial, to Glenn Bowman, Dave Reason, Roger Cardinal, John Jervis, Howard Davis, Stephen Bann, Ben Brewster, Kevin Robins, Fred Inglis, and the several technicians of what was still then the Audio-Visual Services, as well as many others, but the dedication particularly records an on-going indebtedness and evokes memories of several exploratory roads travelled together over more than three decades.

B.S.

1st May 2015

Critical Paranoia by T. E. Worden

Reviewed by Frank Maxwall.

I once read 50,000 titles in one year. Not books, just the titles. I was a reviews editor for a small journal and my job involved a meticulous monthly scanning of the *Bookseller*, in a frequently futile attempt to spot forthcoming books the journal should review. One year of it was quite enough.

Professor Worden's book was perhaps conceived in the grind of a similar task. His introductory chapter is shaped around a quotation from William Godwin, writing in 1831 but looking back to his childhood, when he was apparently prone to ask himself, in terror and anxiety: 'When I have read through all the books that have been written, what shall I do afterwards?' Professor Worden reminds us that in the 1830s fewer than 2000 new books were published annually in Great Britain. Godwin could therefore have kept himself permanently amused by restricting his reading to a mere five a day. By 1900, however, he would have needed to average twenty-five a day to fulfil his primary ambition. Even if he only relaxed with three-deckers three times daily it would have taken him some thirty-six years to consume the 40,000 (or so) works of fiction published during Her Imperial Majesty's reign.

Such calculations are catching. I have just idled away five minutes by estimating that the truly conscientious Shakespeare scholar would need to read a new doctoral dissertation every week for seventeen years simply to match the manic productivity of American doctoral candidates during the years 1966 to 1983, who between them actually managed to start (or finish) a fresh Shakespeare thesis every week. A certain problem of logistics looms however: surely doctoral candidates are by definition, or regulation, themselves conscientious, so how did any of them ever find enough time free from reading all the others' to write their own? One rather pities the graduate who began work in the dying days of 1983: it would be circa 2000 AD before he or she could put pen to paper.

The first main chapter of *Critical Paranoia* is indeed entitled 'Research Paranoia', but it rather gently skirts the pincer-like directives governing that specific breed of harassed thesis-writers, who are still solemnly assured both that they should have read 'all the relevant material' and that the result should be their 'own work'. Professor Worden's concern is more general, or more personal. He instances his own efforts to write a book on James Joyce. Yes, Joyce! He sensibly abandoned it. But only after he had devoted presumably precious research time to concocting a 'computer-aided guesstimate' (Professor Worden is himself, it would seem, the product of an American Graduate School), adding together Joyce's own 'life-time reading-time' and the ditto of Joyce's major critics and commentators, 'allowing for the multiplier-effect of location within the differential generational levels of a dominant commentary-tradition'.

Deciphering this quaint idiom, I conclude that he tried to calculate how long it took Joyce to read all the books he read, how long it took the first 'generation' of Joyce critics to read all the books they read, in preparation for their commentaries, then the second (who would have to read the first), and so on. The result, I confess, was of less interest to me (the phrase 'one page-time to the power of eight' merely bemused me) than the stringently suspicious attitude behind the inquiry. I already agree with Professor Worden's saddened conclusion that there is too much Joyce scholarship for any sane man to read—but the sane conclusion is that any sane man simply doesn't, however much he has to take on trust.

Oddly, however, Professor Worden's complaint seems to be that there was too *little* Joyce scholarship available for him to read. I detect traces of some long-unforgotten and unforgiven institutional injury behind his specification of this lament: that the library resources, research grants and faculty travelling expenses were 'wholly inadequate' to enable him to gain access to all the 'relevant material'. I deeply sympathise. My own polytechnic can afford a book-purchasing expenditure of only £5 per annum per student, and I too—if I desired them—would have to pay for the 63-

2

volume *Joyce Archives* out of my own meagre pocket (at $6,000 a set this is not a bargain I contemplate).

I also respond, perhaps less merely masochistically, to the Professor's next reason ('excuse' would be over-harsh) for abandoning his Joyce book: that the published texts are unreliable. I well remember, as an eager first-year, stumbling across an awesomely eminent Joyce critic on the steps of the Martello Tower; I blushingly acknowledged that, yes, I was just setting my first tentative foot on the North Face of *Finnegans Wake:* 'Take Care,' said he, 'there are at least 700 misprints in the current Random printing.' I humbly confess to not having discovered a single one to this day. But his lofty remark (securely roped as he was to the Manuscripts) rather spoilt my relish even for a harmlessly pleasing sentence in *Araby*: 'I felt the house in bad humour and walked slowly towards the school' (current Penguin printing) — perhaps it wasn't, after all, a gentle Joycean joke but just a genuine misprint.

Professor Worden's own mean-minded contribution to spoiling my enjoyment of Joyce is to inform me that my favourite copy of *Ulysses* contains some 4000 misprints. After such knowledge, it is difficult to forgive him for quoting a phrase from *Ulysses* as the epigraph to this very chapter:

Reading two pages apiece of seven books every night, eh?

Am I *meant* to detect some minute misprint, or am I to be allowed to relax into the rhythmically reverent alliterative echoes of proverbial wisdom?

If there truly is some tiny departure from the best manuscripts here, I can reassure Professor Worden that it escapes me. Apparently he needs such reassurance, since he sums up his chapter with what is surely a *sotto voce* appeal for clemency:

> The inescapable professional dilemma of the academic researcher arises from the inexorable requirement of productivity combined with the advance recognition of inevitable vulnerability. The paranoid reaction to one's

own publication is that, always, somebody out there knows more than I do, and knew it before I did, and that precisely that somebody will be—my reviewer.

Well, he doesn't. Professor Worden.

The second chapter also sports an epigraph from *Ulysses*, the second sentence of 'Proteus':

Signatures of all things I am here to read, seaspawn and seawrack, the nearing tide, that rusty boot.

The chapter is entitled 'Significance Paranoia'. (I would myself have preferred 'That Rusty Boot'—but that is *not* a criticism, Professor Worden.) The aspect of paranoia prominent here is not the projection of hostility but the super-sensitive response to every casual gesture as indicative of vast conspiracies: the paranoid sees significance in *everything*. So does the modern literary critic, according to Professor Worden. Or more strictly perhaps, the post-Modernist (literary) critic.

The coincidence of the professionalisation of academic criticism with the highpoint of Modernism reinforced the notion (endemic to criticism) that texts *need* 'interpretation', down to the last comma, faced with the saturated, polymathic, polysemic, encyclopaedic productions of Joyce, Pound, Eliot, Jones, McDiarmid, Zukovsky and so on, the ordinary easygoing reader had to be transfigured into Super-Reader, knowing that whatever didn't make sense really did and whatever did made more of it than you thought. Watsons were re-trained as Holmeses. Professor Worden is less concerned with the aetiology of this creature than with its current habits and habitat. He tracks the beast first to Paris, offering his own analysis of the shared significance of Lacan's analysis of Poe's *The Purloined Letter* (including the comma—one notes, incidentally, that Lacan's doctoral dissertation was on: paranoia), Barthes's *S/Z* (including that slash), and Derrida's pinpointing of '*hama*' in Aristotle's *Physics* (including the rough breathing). It is not only the microscopic textual focusing he underlines but also the initial selection of 'insignificant' texts and insignificant

4

moments within those texts—most gloriously exemplified in Derrida's disquisition upon Nietzsche's marginal memorandum: 'I have forgotten my umbrella. '

It is this second facet that he sees as significantly similar to an ostensibly traditional tendency: the ever-accelerating resuscitation of minor, marginal and forgotten authors as PhDs dig deeper into the *DNB* for untouched topics, the maniacal meticulousness of dedicated editorial teams aiming asymptotically for the definitive collected works of everybody (where else did Nietzsche's memo come from?), the proliferation of 'critical editions' with a page of apparatus per line of poem (he reproduces an extract from the *Dunciad* at this point). With a certain maliciousness he assimilates these highly respectable endeavours to the fashionably disreputable manoeuvres of those who read texts 'symptomatically' to disclose precisely what is 'absent' from them, since the root of both procedures he finally locates neither in professionalism nor in post-post-Modernism but in Freud's education of an epoch into seeing even the slip of a pen as requiring and rewarding an entire lovume of commentary.

A brief chapter on 'Epistemological Paranoia' is less successful, less amusing, less sure perhaps of its target. It covers the recent ripples of exultant or despairing scepticism, the 'eclipses' and 'destructions' of reason, the essays 'against' method and 'against' epistemology itself, the deconstructionists and the dadaists. It is not that he is himself sceptical about this scepticism; rather, he argues that since any search for systematic and rigorous knowledge is itself a paranoid ambition, an attempt to connect everything which must finally be delusional, correspondingly the repudiation of system in favour of fragment, of rigid grid for rhetorical gesture, betokens a paranoiac self-defence, an attempt to destroy what is still believed in as threatening.

He is mildly more persuasive, I think, when he pinpoints this particular ambivalence in the familiar practice of researchers: the endlessly evasive methodological preliminaries, the continually procrastinated prologemona to a contribution towards a possible model of tentatively partial 'beginnings'. The exact obverse of this super-cautious hesitation is, presumably, the gratuitous option of starting one's analysis just anywhere at all: a comma, a fragment, a footnote, a margin, a full stop.

Paradigms

It is in the light of this triple paranoia that Professor Worden next moves to a rather over-caustic examination of what he seizes upon as 'popular paradigms' in recent academic criticism. He surveys marxism, structuralism, psychoanalysis, deconstruction etc., and then asks what they have in common.

His basic, even brutal, answer is that an allegiance to any of these currents at least mitigates that aspect of research paranoia which has to do with library resources. He argues, with some persuasive examples, that in much marxist criticism the chosen text has been 'related' only to a 'history' composed of little more than half-a-dozen references to an approved group of modem marxist historians (he should, of course, have acknowledged the genuine exceptions), while the plethora of Barthesian, Lacanian and Derridean 'readings' he characterises as 'solving' the problem of 'originality' by merely finding a text that no-one else has yet got around to treating in that particular mode.

Again, his point (he claims) is not to criticise the quality or to query the validity of such work, but to emphasise—as a form of explanation—its convenient material pre-conditions: that such work can be done upon the basis of very restricted resources. Few individuals, or even libraries, have large quantities of, say, sixteenth-century song-books, seventeenth-century pamphlets, eighteenth-century periodicals or nineteenth-century popular fiction—the prerequisites of an older fashion for historical criticism—but even a poor polytechnic's grant allows the purchase of the latest theoretical paradigm-texts. One can fruitfully work from one's own desk copies of *Gawain* and, say, Kristeva (any slur upon an existing Kristevan critique of the Green Knight is, one hopes, unintended), just as—within a previous paradigm —all one really needed were the words upon the page and a dog-eared *Revaluation*.

The obverse of this development has, however, been a further intensification of 'significance paranoia': *every* word, or comma, upon the page must yield its maximum contribution, to maintain continuous production. (It is an intriguing implication of this argument that those disgruntled conservatives who castigate the current vogues should campaign vigorously for an urgent increase in government grants to college libraries.)

With mild and perhaps forgiveable irony, Professor Worden concludes this section of his book with a detailed summary of some recent Joyce criticism founded upon and exemplifying the notion that the (concept) 'author' is dead— and then deploys the 63 volumes of the *Joyce Archive* (his salary is obviously larger than mine) to trace the minutely deliberated construction by Joyce, in notes, drafts, revisions, amendments, proof-corrections, of every quotation employed in an influential book premissed upon the dissociation of any 'reading' of Joyce-texts from Joyce's own intentions in writing. His predictable motto for this exercise is Joyce's own remark.

I've put in so many enigmas and puzzles that it will keep the professors busy for centuries arguing over what I meant.

Yet despite the relish of Professor Worden's critique, one may still remind him that arguing over 'what *I* meant' is precisely *not* what many critics now do. Nor do I see any *a priori* necessity why they should. Indeed, in his final section the Professor himself endorses quite other priorities.

Clinical Paranoia

First, however, he steps back from his engagement with recent critical practices and devotes a long chapter to an examination of the term he has thus far rather loosely employed: 'paranoia'. As he recognises, one might be tempted to categorise many of the phenomena he has listed under the term 'obsessional neurosis' rather than 'paranoia'. Professor Worden's reply is twofold: that though individual critics may be justly described as obsessional neurotics, the 'discipline' of criticism is more usefully thought of as 'paranoid in structure', and, secondly, that a neurotic symptom may in any case be the 'nucleus' of a psychosis. He quotes Freud's 1917 *Introductory Lectures:*

> For a symptom of an 'actual' neurosis is often the nucleus and first stage of a psycho-neurotic symptom. A relation of this kind can be most clearly observed between neurasthenia and the transference neurosis known as 'conversion hysteria', between anxiety neurosis and anxiety hysteria, but also between hypochondria and the forms of disorder which will be mentioned later under the name of paraphrenia (dementia praecox and paranoia).

On this basis, he feels free to utilise Freud's characterisation of obsessional neurosis in order to specify more exactly what he means by 'Critical Paranoia'. For example, he cites a number of passages from the 'Rat Man' case which he offers as paralleling aspects of 'epistemological paranoia':

> Another mental need, which is . . . shared by obsessional neurotics, . . . is the need for *uncertainty* in their life, or for *doubt.* Their essential characteristic is that they are incapable of coming to a decision . . ; they endeavour to postpone every decision . . .

> In the various forms of obsessional neurosis in which the epistemophilic instinct plays a part, its relation to thought-processes makes it particularly well-adapted to attract the energy which is vainly endeavouring to make its way forward into action, and divert it into the sphere of thought, where there is a possibility of its obtaining pleasurable satisfaction of another sort. . . .

> But procrastination in *action* is soon replaced by lingering over *thoughts* . . . in other words, an obsessive or compulsive thought is one whose function it is to represent an act regressively.

Somewhat unkindly in my view, Professor Worden at this point quotes from Jacques Derrida *(Marges,* p. 207) on 'undecidability':

> There is, then, probably no choice to be made between two lines of thought; our task is rather to reflect on the circularity which makes the one pass into the other indefinitely.

But, as he also explicitly acknowledges, a desire for action (as in Derrida's case) remains at the root of obsessional displacement, and to retain that desire—however unconsciously inhibited or externally blocked—may be preferable to inert acquiescence in inaction.

In a very early note *(Draft N* of *Project for a Scientific Psychology,* 1897), Freud had recognised one feature of paranoia as 'pathological distrust of rulers and monarchs', but distrust of rulers may not be pathological. Freud's later admission that paranoid jealousy may even disclose a certain truth perhaps has its political counterpart:

> These attacks [of paranoid jealousy] drew their material from his observation of minute indications, by which his wife's quite unconscious coquetry, unnoticeable to any one else, had betrayed itself to him. . . . He was extraordinarily observant of all these manifestations of her unconscious, and always knew how to interpret them correctly, so that he really was in the right about it. . . . His abnormality really reduced itself to this, that he watched his wife's unconscious mind much more closely and then regarded it as far more important than anyone else would have thought of doing.

Professor Worden offers in fact his own variation of this suggestion, noting that even Schreber's delusions of world catastrophe have a ring of truth in a nuclear age and that, as in Freud's analysis of Schreber, such a 'delusion . . . which we take to be the pathological product, is in reality an attempt at recovery, a process of reconstruction'—or at least may in the case of 'correct' political 'paranoia' be a step *towards* sanity. But such considerations are a sidetrack from his main argument, where he has to confront a major difficulty.

If Professor Worden wants to maintain that the modern discipline of criticism is 'paranoid in structure', that the professional practitioners of criticism (whatever their personal psychic state of health) enter into an endemically paranoid discourse characterised by pro-crastination, obsessional displacement, delusions of persecution, megalomania, undecid-ability, intrinsic uncertainty, and even pathological jealousy (it's unclear how many of Freud's own sub-categories he would apply), then what is the aetiology of this curious discourse?

For Freud, the origins of paranoia are always to be found in 'a secondary narcissism which is a return of the original infantile one' and which takes the form of a repressed libidinal attachment of a passive homosexual character, against which the paranoid is defending him- or her-self. Yet though it might be amusing to speculate on the relevance of this insight to the biographies of individual critics, it is hardly intelligible that the character of a 'discipline' might be explained along such lines.

Foreclosure

Professor Worden's solution to this dilemma is to reject Freud's explanation and to rely instead upon Jacques Lacan. Commenting upon Mrs. Macalpine's introductory analysis in her edition of Schreber's *Memoirs,* Lacan wrote (with his usual lucidity):

> Her critique of the cliché that is confined in the factor of the repression of a homosexual drive, which, in fact, is quite unclear, to explain psychosis, is quite masterly, and she demonstrates this beautifully in the Schreber case itself. Homosexuality, supposedly a determinant of paranoiac psychosis, is really a symptom articulated in its process.

But Lacan is then under an obligation to offer an alternative aetiology of this 'process'. He does so by proposing a general distinction between neurosis and psychosis. Neurosis arises from 'repression' but psychosis from 'repudiation'—respectively *Verdrängung* and *Verwerfung* in Freud's German; the latter term is *forclusion'* in Lacan's French and can also be translated 'foreclosure'. Professor Worden quotes from a disciple of Lacan (Monsieur Laplanche) to clarify the distinction:

> If we imagine experience to be a piece of material made up of crisscrossing threads, we could say that repression would figure in it as a rent or tear which can still be repaired, whereas foreclosure would figure in it as a *béance* [abyss, gap, nothing] due to the weaving itself, in short a primal hole which will never again be able to find its substance, since it has never been anything other than the substance of a hole and can only be filled, and even then imperfectly, by a patch.

Professor Worden tries to elucidate this obscure distinction further, by pursuing the intricacies of Lacan's theory of psychosis and his specifications of the differences between, for example, schizophrenia and delusional paranoia.

I found the details of this exploration both difficult and unnecessary, for the same basic reason: since I am neither analyst nor analysand, I would myself have no assured basis upon which to assess the validity of Lacan's argument. In any case, Professor Worden is trying to illuminate the character of literary criticism and I have to judge *that* attempt according to whether the analytic distinctions he finally develops, whatever their validity elsewhere, do coherently clarify the state of criticism for me. So I decline to follow him into the less-than- fascinating entrails of *Ecrits*. I will, however, single out three further passages he cites, since they provide some of the terms of his later discussion. One is from *The Language of Psychoanalysis* by Laplanche and Pontalis, stating that 'foreclosure' consists in a primordial expulsion of a fundamental signifier (e.g. the phallus as signifier of the castration complex) from the subject's Symbolic universe. Foreclosure is deemed to be distinct from repression in two senses:

a. Foreclosed signifiers are not integrated into the subject's unconscious ;

b. They do not return 'from the inside'; they re-emerge, rather, in 'the Real', particularly through the phenomenon of hallucination.

The other two passages are both from Freud himself, where the concept of foreclosure/repudiation seems to be at work, without the explicit terminology:

> There is, however, a much more energetic and successful kind of defence. Here, the ego rejects [*verwirft*] the incompatible idea with its affect and behaves as if the idea had never occurred to the ego at all.

> It was incorrect to say that the perception which was suppressed internally is projected outwards; the truth is rather, as we now see, that what was abolished internally returns from without.

The argument returns to literary criticism with a summary of the conclusion of a recent introductory text-book on literary theory. The gist of this is that the adoption of various theoretical approaches to 'literature' has served to dissolve the very notion of 'literature' itself, since those same approaches apply as readily to the *Daily Mirror* as to *Paradise Lost*, and this cuts both ways, denying simultaneously the specific character of any 'literary' object and of any 'literary' method. Therefore:

> If literary theory presses its own implications too far, then it has argued itself out of existence. . . . The final logical move in a process which began by recognising that literature is an illusion is to recognise that literary theory is an illusion too. It is not of course an illusion in

the sense that I have invented the various people I have discussed in this book. Northrop Frye really does exist and so did F.R. Leavis.

At this point Professor Worden pounces. Once again he summons up a vivid, even moving, picture of what seems to be his favourite habitat: a library. He invites us to consider those massed stacks of packed shelves in the 'Literature' section, all those works by Joyce and his generations of critics. Are *these* an 'illusion', he asks? They very palpably exist, they surround the weighed-down scholar scratching away in his notebook, they confront him as a material reality, a category of concrete knowledge, a professional challenge and an exemplum. (The professor's style modulates into a pained rhetoric which I mitigate.) But what if that scholar has 'repudiated' the very notion of 'literature'? What if the poor researcher never really had a concept of 'literature' in the first place? What if 'literature' were, in short, 'a primal hole which will never again be able to find its substance, since it has never been anything other than the substance of a hole'?

One response might be to 'reject' *this* 'incompatible idea with its affect' and to behave 'as if the idea had never occurred . . . at all.' But even then, perhaps, 'what was abolished internally returns from without'—in those stacks of 'Literature' but also in one's professional identity, qualifications, career, prospects, institutional post—and publications, soon to swell those very stacks.

There seem to be two varieties of this dilemma. The more 'radical' critics are in the most paradoxical position, since 'literature' for them really is acknowledged as a *béance* due to the weaving itself, despite their daily confrontation with its concrete illusion. But others, and among them the most traditional, seem often to have repudiated 'literature' by other means: in seeking to encompass literature within modes of 'knowledge' that are deliberately constructed as distinct in kind from the object of that 'knowledge', they implicitly refuse the notion they proclaim, that literature might be itself a mode of 'knowledge'; in endlessly producing non-'literature' themselves they pay homage to a distinction of status which their very act of supplementation subverts; in writing criticism rather than poems they repudiate the priorities they uphold while implying that the poets should really have provided the necessary criticism in place of the dependent poems; in asserting their own necessity they remove the rationale for their very existence.

Now, speaking personally, I quite enjoyed the passion of Professor Worden's attack in this section, which I have humbly tried to reproduce, in a somewhat briefer compass. Perhaps there is even a faint touch of paranoia in his own (self-) hostility, but I agree that the dilemma he gestures at can indeed be real: one's attachment to literature can at times seem asymptotically structured, a repeated search for that which is always elsewhere than the actual object of one's probing critical attention, a daily discrimination against a norm which itself dissolves under that discrimination.

Yet I take a certain comfort from two comments, one of which I have shamelessly cribbed from Professor Worden himself—his earlier quotation from Derrida:

> There is, then, probably no choice to be made between two lines of thought; our task is rather to reflect on the circularity which makes the one pass into the other indefinitely.

The other is from a *Guardian* review by Raymond Williams of *Anna Karenina and other essays* by that same F. R. Leavis who was no illusion:

> I have indeed found myself thinking of Leavis's critical work as a kind of novel, in which the main events are certain novels and plays, and most of the characters are from fiction and drama... but in which the central consciousness and the central attention is on what he calls in this book 'the lived question': an exploration, a dramatisation, an inward finding and realisation of values through this composed and apparently objective medium.

Oddly, Professor Worden might endorse at least the spirit of Williams' remarks, since he clearly wants to salvage a notion of 'literature' as precisely a distinctive mode, not of 'knowledge', but of attention, even of realisation of values. The pressure for this salvage operation seems to come from two sources, or considerations.

First, and perhaps unconsciously, he clearly doesn't really *want* to read all that Joyce criticism, nor add more of the same: his own procrastination (computer-aided guesstimates indeed!) and his rapid abandonment of the book proclaims it. Second, he nevertheless respects, enjoys and admires Joyce's work. That some criticism might increase or modify such respect and enjoyment he probably wouldn't deny. So how does he himself escape the paranoid trajectory of 'criticism'? One option would be silence. Another, to become Samuel Beckett—and it is surely significant that his epigraph for this section comes from Beckett's *The Unnamable:*

> What have you done with your material? We have left it behind. But commanded to say whether yes or no they filled up the holes, have you filled up the holes yes or no, they will say yes and no, or some yes, others no, at the same time, not knowing what answer the master wants, to his question. But both are defendable.

But the third option, it seems, is to repudiate the notion of literature as a mode of knowledge or even as an object of knowledge, thus rejecting the paranoid urge after knowledge —while retaining a notion of literature as a mode of persuasion and as a means of persuasion.

Triangles and Lines

In the final section of his book Professor Worden elaborates this distinction in terms of an opposition between what he calls 'the critical line' and 'the critical triangle'. The critical triangle is the basic shape of much academic criticism, and it takes two forms.

In the first, the triangle is formed between author, text and reader, with the critic standing 'outside' the triangle. The critic's job from this position is to explicate or explain the text to the reader and to evaluate it for the reader, and sometimes for the author too. If he evaluates it for the author (legislative criticism, reviewing) the critic 'knows' more than the author; if for the reader, then more than the reader. If the critic explicates the text for the reader (elucidates its obscurities) then the critic and probably the author know more than the reader (the critic may appeal here to his knowledge of the author's knowledge). If the critic explains the text (by relating it to its generic tradition, historical context, etc.) the critic knows more than the reader, and perhaps more than the author. In each case, the relations are those of degrees of knowledge, though the contents of that knowledge will vary.

In the second form of academic criticism, the triangle is composed between the text and two readers, and the critic is within the triangle as one (or both) of the readers. Here the essential task, shared by both readers, is to 'know' the text more completely (again, the contents of that knowledge will vary), which may involve various detours into the first kind of critical triangle. There have been different attempts to modify these modes of academic criticism, by substituting or redefining the terms: for example, in contestations over the canon of texts, or the concept of author, or the objects of knowledge. Professor Worden, while responsive to many of these efforts, sees them as basically retaining the triangular shape.

By contrast, his notion of a 'critical line' offers a linear model in which the critic stands in a line with a reader, beyond both of whom the line extends to an *issue*. The task of the critic is to persuade the reader to take an attitude, a direction, towards that issue. But that is also, for Professor Worden, the essential task of a 'literary' text, and also of its author. The text is a means of persuading a reader to take an attitude towards an issue. Author, text, and critic (and reader) may be in agreement concerning the issue and the attitude, or they may not. The critic may use the text, or parts of it, to persuade the reader, perhaps using knowledge about the author, or the author's attitude, to reinforce that persuasion; the attitude of the author or of the text may be contrary to the critic's, but that may itself be used to persuade the reader to take up an attitude against the text's on the issue in question.

But always for Professor Worden what is at stake as the final object of attention in criticism is not the text or the author but, first, an issue (whether one 'acknowledged' by the text or not) and, secondly, an interlocutor, another reader. In that sense, the text is potentially redundant, as indeed are the roles of author, critic and reader: if two people agree about an issue they have no need to discuss 'literature' in relation to that issue. It is perhaps because people often do not agree, about either what is to count as an issue or what attitude to take, that we have found a need for a mode of writing which offers not knowledge but a means of persuasion, and why some modes of writing which did once offer knowledge now survive as literature.

I have tried to be fair to this account, though necessarily simplifying it, and I agree with Professor Worden to this extent, that his notion of a 'critical line' does indeed reflect the way in which we frequently 'use' literature, whether in convenient quotations, urgent recommendations, or dramatic adaptations; moreover, the majority of 'literary texts' may well have been written for purposes of persuasion: to celebrate a victory, support a monarch, seduce a beloved, ridicule an enemy, instil an ideology.

It nevertheless mildly amazes me that, after the recent flurries of impressive theoretical paradigms, a modern Professor of English at a modern university should explicitly propose as the task of criticism what is really a variation upon a long-discredited 'moralism'. Personally, I partly applaud, especially since I suspect most subsequently fashionable modes of in fact operating as disguised moralisms. But I do have one absolute reservation. That great exemplar of a defiantly moralist criticism, Dr Leavis, did indeed want to 'use' (though neither he nor I would endorse that verb) literature to persuade his readers, and pupils, to take up an attitude, and he believed that serious literature shared that aim—but, quite crucially, it was an attitude towards *life* not towards 'issues'. That seems to me a wholly necessary distinction, and one that—if I may so put it —the authorities at Professor Worden's university should bear carefully in mind.

In sum, then, I sympathise to a considerable extent with the dilemma explored and the proposal offered in *Critical Paranoia*, though I remain unconvinced by the precise analysis of that dilemma and I would firmly dissociate myself from some implications of the proposal. Yet in the light of the book's own argument a final question remains. One rather wonders why professor Worden wrote it, rather than telling us what issue should concern us in reading *Finnegans Wake*.

Frank Maxwall

LITERARY VALUE?

I've been asked to talk, in a way that might interest an audience of philosophers, about the relations between marxism and literary criticism, and, more generally, about politics and art. It's a tall order, and as usual there is the problem of how to begin. I'm going to start from a very simple point and see where it leads me.

Marx's critique of political economy and literary criticism have, on the face of it, one term at least in common, the term 'value'. In the discussion of literature, at some point or other, the notion of 'literary value' will come into play. And in the first couple of pages of *Capital* Marx sets up a distinction which underpins a great deal of his analysis: the distinction between 'use-value' and 'exchange-value'. If we begin from Marx's use of those terms and pursue them with an eye on 'literary value', it might be interesting to see whether we ever arrive at some connection between the two.

Let me summarise Marx's distinction between use-value and exchange-value by quoting two paragraphs from Capital which make the basic points clearly enough:

> The usefulness of a thing makes it a use-value. But this usefulness does not dangle in mid-air. It is conditioned by the physical properties of the commodity, and has no existence apart from the latter. It is therefore the physical body of the commodity itself, for instance iron, corn, a diamond, which is the use-value or useful thing. This property of a commodity is independent of the amount of labour required to appropriate its useful qualities . . . Use-values are only realised in use or in consumption. They constitute the material content of wealth, whatever its social form may be. In the form of society to be considered here they are also the material bearers of exchange-value.

> Exchange-value appears first of all as the quantitative relation, the proportion, in which use-values of one kind exchange for use-values of another kind. This relation

changes constantly with time and place. Hence exchange-value appears to be something accidental and purely relative, and consequently an intrinsic value, i.e. an exchange-value that is inseparably connected with the commodity, inherent in it, seems a contradiction in terms.

That distinction seems clear enough—at first. But there is an intriguing moment in his writings when Marx suddenly asks himself a basic question about those terms. In the notebooks of drafts for *Capital*—the *Grundrisse* —we find the following:

> The use-value which the worker has to offer to the capitalist, which he has to offer to others in general, is not materialised in a product, does not exist apart from him at all, thus exists not really, but only in potentiality, as his capacity. It becomes a reality only when it has been solicited by capital, is set in motion, since activity without object is nothing, or, at the most, mental activity, which is not the question at issue here. As soon as it has obtained motion from capital, this use-value exists as the worker's specific, productive activity; it is his vitality itself, directed toward a specific purpose and hence expressing itself in a specific form.
>   In the relation of capital and labour, exchange-value and use-value are brought into relation; the one side (capital) initially stands opposite the other side as exchange-value,

Suddenly at this point, interrupting the flow, there is a long note by Marx, a side-thought or marginal jotting, which I want to quote the beginning of:

> Is not value to be conceived of as the unity of use-value and exchange-value? In and for itself, is value as such the general form, in opposition to use-value and exchange-value as particular forms of it? Does this have significance in economics? Use-value presupposed even in simple exchange or barter. But here, where exchange

takes place only for the reciprocal use of the commodity, the use-value, i.e. the content, the natural particularity of the commodity has as such no standing as an economic form. Its form, rather, is exchange-value. The content apart from this form is irrelevant; is not a content of the relation as a social relation. But does this content as such not develop into a system of needs and production? Does not use-value as such enter into the form itself, as a determinant of the form itself, e.g. in the relation of capital and labour? the different forms of labour?—agriculture, industry, etc.—ground rent?—effect of the seasons on raw product prices ? etc. If only exchange-value as such plays a role in economics, then how could elements later enter which relate purely to use-value, such as, right away, in the case of capital as raw material etc.? How is it that the physical composition of the soil suddenly drops out of the sky in Ricardo?

Apart from its fascination as an example of Marx struggling with an apparent blockage in his own thinking, this tortuously probing passage has a particular interest if we think of 'literary value'. For if we try to apply the terms 'use-value' and 'exchange-value' to literature, one might suggest that exchange-value would refer to, if nothing else, the market-value of a book, a book as an object (a line of thought that might bring into play first-editions, and manuscripts, as well as the price of a new book), or perhaps the economic value of an established literary reputation (a Nobel Prize is worth a great deal to the recipient's publisher). But 'use-value' is a bit trickier, even at first glance, since, as Marx says himself, 'Every useful thing is a whole composed of many properties; it can therefore be useful in various ways'.

As a physical object, a book, Shakespeare's works can be useful in a variety of ways: as a paper-weight, a doorstop, a missile, etc. And even as that curious thing 'a play', Hamlet can be 'useful' as a way of passing an evening, as a means of employment for actors or profit for a theatre management, or as a mine of quotable lines. Somehow, one wants to say, its 'literary value' isn't to be equated with any of these. One might be tempted to push in the same direction as Marx's note and ask something like: 'is literary value as such the general form, in opposition to some of these use-values as particular forms of it?' Or one might even want to extend Marx's question and ask: 'is value as such the general form, in opposition to use-value, exchange-value, and literary-value as particular forms of it?' I suspect that both these questions, and indeed Marx's own term 'value as such', would lead to dead-ends if explored further.

But it's not, I think, an accident that this question—what is 'value'?—strikes Marx in connection with a passage that mentions, *en passant*, that 'activity without object is nothing, or, at the most, mental activity, which is not the question at issue here,' since Marx's notion of use-value seems to be tied to physical objects: 'It is therefore the physical body of the commodity itself, for instance iron, corn, a diamond, which is the use-value or useful thing.' Yet as soon as one thinks of the 'value' of Marx's own thinking, for example, it seems slightly odd to restrict that 'value' to the 'physical body of the commodity itself, even if we recognise that writing, or 'thinking', is a physical activity and the product of writing is a material thing. For it is not any particular material thing (this copy of *Hamlet*, this edition of *Capital*), as such, that we are interested in. More generally, we could put the problem in these terms: how is the term 'use-value' related to intellectual labour or imaginative creation?

In a curious way, the marginal note in the *Grundrisse* already looks forward to the context in which Marx himself toys further with this problem. The note begins to tussle with Ricardo at the point where I left off quoting it. Much of Marx's detailed analysis of Ricardo and other political economists is to be found in the papers known as *Theories of Surplus Value*. In a section of notes concerned with 'Theories of productive and unproductive labour', Marx makes some comments on Henri Storch's *Cours d'economie politique*, particularly about Storch's views on 'spiritual production', 'the elements of civilisation', 'immaterial values', or what he calls 'internal goods'—i.e. that area of activity we might now call 'culture'. Marx writes:

According to Storch, the physician 'produces' health (but also illness), professors and writers produce enlightenment (but also obscurantism), poets, painters, etc., produce morals, preachers religion, the sovereign's labour security, and so on. It can just as well be said that illness produces physicians, stupidity produces professors and writers, lack of taste poets and painters, immorality moralists, superstition preachers and general insecurity produces the sovereign. This way of saying in fact that all these activities, these services, produce a real or imaginary use-value is repeated by later writers in order to prove that they are productive workers in Adam Smith's sense, that is to say, that they directly produce not products *sui generis* but products of material labour and consequently immediate wealth.

It's fairly clear from this that Marx regards Storch, and others, as mistaken when they draw terms from the field of political economy and attempt to use them in the field of 'culture' as if those terms could simply mean the same in the two different regions. And one corollary of that misapplication is the tendency to justify cultural work in illegitimate ways. It would seem from this passage, at least, that Marx would look rather coldly on any attempt to link directly the use of the term 'value' in his critique of political economy and the use of the same word in literary criticism—just as he might well regard as slipshod and Storch-like the currently fashionable use of phrases such as 'intellectual production', 'theoretical production', 'literary production'.

Marx's own notion of productive labour is made clear enough in another passage from *Theories of Surplus Value*, which, interestingly, uses literary activities as an example:

The same kind of labour may be productive or unproductive. For example, Milton, who wrote *Paradise Lost* for five pounds, was an unproductive labourer. On the other hand, the writer who turns out stuff for his publisher in factory style, is a productive labourer.

Milton produced *Paradise Lost* for the same reason that a silk worm produces silk. It was an activity of his nature. Later he sold the product for £5. But the literary proletarian of Leipzig, who fabricates books (for example, Compendia of Economics) under the direction of his publisher, is a productive labourer; for his product is from the outset subsumed under capital, and comes into being only for the purpose of increasing that capital. A singer who sells her song for her own account is an unproductive labourer. But the same singer commissioned by an entrepreneur to sing in order to make money for him is a productive labourer; for she produces capital.

The problem of the distinction between productive and unproductive labour is, for Marx, an aspect of the broader problem of the division of labour, and in *Capital*, I, chapter 14, he makes this general comment about historically distinct ways of thinking about the division of labour:

> Political economy, which first emerged as an independent science during the period of manufacture, is only able to view the social division of labour in terms of the division found in manufacture, i.e. as a means of producing more commodities with a given quantity of labour, and consequently of cheapening commodities and accelerating the accumulation of capital. In most striking contrast with this accentuation of quantity and exchange-value is the attitude of the writers of classical antiquity, who are exclusively concerned with quality and use-value. As a result of the separation of the social branches of production, commodities are better made, men's various inclinations and talents select suitable fields of action, and without some restriction no important results can be obtained anywhere. Hence both product and producer are improved by the division of labour. If the growth of the quantity produced is occasionally mentioned, this is only done with reference to the greater abundance of use-values. There is not a word alluding to exchange-value, or to the cheapening

of commodities. This standpoint, the standpoint of use-value, is adopted by Plato, who treats the division of labour as the foundation on which the division of society into estates is based.

This reference to Plato is backed up by a footnote, which reads:

With Plato, the division of labour within the community develops from the many-sidedness of the needs of individuals, and the one-sidedness of their capabilities. The main point with him is that the labourer must adapt himself to the work, not the work to the labourer, a thing which would be unavoidable if the labourer carried on several trades at once, thus making one or the other of them subordinate.

Marx then quotes a supporting passage from Plato's *Republic*, Book II, 370C. It's from part of the initial stages in the argument that is to dominate the whole *Republic*: Socrates has suggested that if they are to find the answer to the question of whether 'justice' is 'better' than 'injustice', they should look first at the nature of justice in the State, and this involves examining initially the 'origin of the city'—the reason why the State exists—which is 'the fact that we do not severally suffice for our own needs, but each of us lacks many things' and therefore 'one man calling in another for one service and another for another, we, being in need of many things, gather many into one place of abode as associates and helpers, and to this dwelling together we give the name of city or State' (369B).

I want to use this reference to Plato's argument by Marx in order to leave Marx himself for a while. Since Marx doesn't discuss the problem of literary value himself (in this kind of context, at any rate), it might be as well to look at Plato, who implicitly does, and then perhaps return to Marx with some clearer questions.

If therefore we now look at Plato's case against 'poets' in Book III of *Republic*, we find that he brings into play, as one step in his argument, precisely the point about the 'one-sidedness' of a man's capacities which Marx noted, but Plato elaborates it in an intriguing way. At 394E, he has Socrates say:

> This, then, Adeimantus, is the point we must keep in view, do we wish our guardians to be good mimics or not? Or is this also a consequence of what we said before, that each one could practise well only one pursuit and not many, but if he attempted the latter, dabbling in many things, he would fail of distinction in all?

The reference back to 370C is clear, but it's also worth referring back to the original question which began this whole section about poets. At 376C Socrates, having established the kind of 'character' required in the ruling 'guardians' of the ideal republic, had asked: 'But the rearing of these men and their education, how shall we manage that?' The inquiry that follows is therefore to do with how the guardians will be educated; in our terms, we might formulate the question as: who is to educate them, and what should they read? In the rest of Book II Plato establishes that some poets sometimes 'tell lies about the gods' and that Book concludes:

> When anyone says that sort of thing about the gods, we shall be wroth with him, we will refuse him a chorus, neither will we allow teachers to use him for the education of the young if our guardians are to be god-fearing men and god-like insofar as that is possible for humanity.

On Plato's premisses, the conclusion seems fair enough: if poetry is like this it shouldn't be used in educating the guardians. But if we return to 394E the problem seems, at first, to have changed, for there Socrates seems to be asking whether the guardians should be poets, not merely whether they should read them: 'do we wish our guardians to be good mimics or not?' The Loeb translation, which I've been quoting, retains the sense of the Greek by using 'mimics' for '*mimetikous*'. Other translations at this point have, for example, 'Do we want our guardians to be capable of playing many parts?' (Cornford) or 'capable of playing many characters' (H. D. P. Lee).

The difficulty of translation arises partly because the Greek word which is at the root of this notion of 'mimicking' is *mimeomai* (the verb) or *mimesis* (the noun), and these words, and their derivative forms, are normally translated into English as 'imitate' and 'imitation', the implication being that to 'imitate' is to produce an 'imitation', a copy of something, a representation. The word 'mimesis' has, I suppose, become familiar enough in English, if only through the title of Auerbach's famous book. But I think we tend to presume too quickly that 'mimesis' has only one meaning; we think of 'mimesis' in terms of, say, a painting being a representation of something, but if we think of 'mimesis' as meaning also a 'mimicking', it's clear that we don't think of a painting as 'mimicking' its subject. Let's pursue Plato's use of the word a bit further by going back to the beginning of his discussion of what we would probably call 'literary form'. At 392D, we have this:

> 'Do not they [fabulists or poets] proceed either by pure narration or by a narrative that is effected through imitation or by both?' 'This too,' he said, 'I still need to have made plainer.' 'I seem to be a ridiculous and obscure teacher,' I said; 'so like men who are unable to express themselves I won't try to speak in wholes and universals but will separate off a particular part and by the example of that try to show you my meaning. Tell me. Do you know the first lines of the *Iliad* in which the poet says that Chryses implored Agamemnon to release his daughter, and that the king was angry and that Chryses, failing of his request, imprecated curses on the Achaeans in his prayers to the god?' 'I do.' 'You know then that as far as these verses,

> And prayed unto all the Achaeans,
> Chiefly to Atreus' sons, twin leaders who marshalled
>   the people,

the poet himself is the speaker and does not even attempt to suggest to us that anyone but himself is speaking. But what follows he delivers as if he were himself Chryses and tries as far as may be to make us feel that not Homer is the speaker, but the priest, an old man. And in this manner he has carried on nearly all the rest of his narration about affairs in Ilion, all that happened in Ithaca, and the entire Odyssey.' 'Quite so,' he said. 'Now, it is narration, is it not, both when he presents the several speeches and the matter between the speeches?' 'Of course.' 'But when he delivers a speech as if he were someone else, shall we not say that he then assimilates thereby his own diction as far as possible to that of the person whom he announces as about to speak?' 'We shall obviously.' 'And is not likening one's self to another in speech or bodily bearing an imitation of him to whom one likens one's self?' 'Surely.' 'In such case then, it appears, he and the other poets effect their narration   through imitation.' 'Certainly.' 'But if the poet should conceal himself nowhere, then his entire poetising and narration would have been accomplished without imitation.'

The distinction, as it's used here, between 'narration' (*diegesis*) with and without 'imitation' (*mimesis*) may strike us as clear enough in itself, but we might still feel that to use 'imitation' in this sense is slightly odd. The Loeb translation has a footnote which tries to explain, but it seems to me still caught in a particular notion of what 'imitation' means in English:

> All art is essentially imitation for Plato and Aristotle. But imitation means for them not only the portrayal or description of visible and tangible things, but more especially the communication of a mood or feeling, hence the (to a modern) paradox that music is the most imitative of the arts. But Plato here complicates the

matter further by sometimes using imitation in the narrower sense of dramatic dialogue as opposed to narration.

I don't think Plato is 'complicating the matter' by his use of *mimesis* here (which the Loeb translates by 'imitation'); indeed it's arguable that this use of *mimesis* is a very ordinary one for a Greek. Cornford, in a note in his translation, puts the point very clearly:

> Plato now passes from the content of literature used in school to its form. The Greek schoolboy was not allowed to repeat Homer or Aeschylus in a perfunctory gabble, but expected to throw himself into the story and deliver the speeches with the tones and gesture of an actor. (The professional reciter. Ion, describes how, when he was reciting Homer, his eyes watered and his hair stood on end, *Ion* 535C.) The word for this dramatic representation is *mimesis*. This has also the wider sense of 'imitation', and towards the end of this section it is used of the realistic copying of natural sounds and noises in music. But at first Plato is chiefly concerned with the actor's assumption of a character. The actor does not 'imitate' Othello, whom he has never seen; he represents or embodies or reproduces the character created by Shakespeare. In some degree the spectator also identifies himself with a character he admires. Plato held that, in childhood particularly, such imaginative identification may leave its permanent mark on the characters of actor and audience.

We can perhaps see more clearly now why it is that Plato can argue from *this* notion of *mimesis* towards his conclusion at 395C; neither 'mimic' nor 'imitate' seems quite right (we seem to need a term like 'mimate'), but if we substitute 'mimic' for 'imitate' in the Loeb translation the argument at 395C might recover some of its force:

> If, then, we are to maintain our original principle, that our guardians, released from all other crafts, are to be

expert craftsmen of civil liberty, and pursue nothing else that does not conduce to this, it would not be fitting for these to do nor yet to *mimic* anything else. But if they mimic they should from childhood up mimic what is appropriate to them—men, that is, who are brave, sober, pious, free and all things of that kind: but things unbecoming the free man they should neither do nor be clever at mimicking, nor yet any other shameful thing, lest from the mimicking they absorb the reality. Or have you not observed that mimicking, if continued from youth far into life, settles down into habits and (second) nature in the body, the speech, and the thought?

What I'm suggesting, therefore, is that the idea of 'throwing oneself into the part', of temporarily 'becoming' the character who is speaking in the text, is crucial to an understanding of Plato's argument about the relations between literature, education, and the 'politics' of his republic. This rather neglected element in Plato's objections to certain kinds of literature could lead us in various directions. For example, it might illuminate his own literary form! It could also help us to make sense of Plato's notion of what happens when a poet composes poetry, as in the famous passage in *Laws* 719C:

> Whenever a poet is seated on the Muses' tripod, he is not in his senses, but resembles a fountain, which gives free course to the upward rush of water; and, since his art consists of *mimesis*, he is compelled often to contradict himself, when he creates characters of contradictory moods; and he knows not which of these contradictory utterances is true.

I think Plato means 'contradict himself' rather literally; insofar as the poet 'becomes' each character in turn, he does suffer something like a split self, a self in contra-diction with itself. And it should now be clear that for Plato reading can involve a similar kind of *mimesis*—an assumption of another 'self', a process of being a 'mimic'. Which should bring us back to 'literature'.

But in fact I want at this point to take a sudden jump to what may seem an entirely unrelated subject: film criticism. What interests me here—and will eventually connect back to Plato—is that recent work in film-criticism, particularly, has tried to make use of certain notions drawn from Jacques Lacan's version of psychoanalysis, and one fundamental reason for that utilisation of Lacan has been that Lacanian psychoanalysis seems to suggest ways in which marxism and the 'theory of the subject' can be brought critically together.

Let me expand that a bit. Most of the writers associated with the film journal *Screen* have sought to establish a connection between marxism and film-analysis, but the kind of marxism they prefer—basically that inspired by Louis Althusser—emphasises the key role of 'the subject' as the core-notion of ideology: to think in terms of individual human subjects, coherently unified individuals as the sources of meanings, the originators of action and discourse, is to think ideologically—to fail to recognise that the 'individual' is an ensemble of social relations, and that action and discourse are to be accounted for in terms of systems of relations (of production, of meaning, of significance) which are dominant over and actually constitute or construct the 'individual' and of which that 'individual' is largely ignorant or necessarily unconscious. I'm obviously simplifying, drastically, a complex and difficult case, but the case as a whole is not my concern at the moment. I want here simply to pick up some of the Lacanian notions that have been put to work in film-theory and then, later, suggest some possible parallels or applications in the field of 'literature'—which might, by a few crab-like steps, allow us then to return to.Marx.

Let me begin with some standard classifications in film-theory. One can distinguish three different ways in which 'looking' is involved in a normal 'narrative' or 'fiction' film. First, the camera is 'looking' at something, whatever is in the field of vision of the lens at the time of filming—the 'pro-filmic event' which is filmed. Second, the audience in the cinema 'looks' at the screen, it watches the film. Third, in a typical commercial movie, the characters in the 'story' (the diegesis, what the narrative of the film unfolds) 'look' at each other. A fourth 'look', rare in commercial cinema, occurs when the audience is 'looked' at by a figure on the screen; Jean-Luc Godard might be instanced as a director who makes use of scenes involving a 'look' that approximates to this 'fourth look'.

The implications of these distinctions between different 'looks' have been explored in a variety of directions: e.g. the way most commercial films try to ensure that the audience remains unaware of the fact of the camera, or even of the screen; the audience, on the other hand, becomes preoccupied with the 'looks' of the characters. The distinction between these different 'looks' can to a certain extent be paralleled in at least one instance of painting.

Michel Foucault, in his *Les mots et les choses*, has analysed Velasquez's painting *Las Meninas* in a way that can be adapted for my purposes here. We look at the painting. We see the interior of a room, in which the 'maids of honour' of the title are clustered round Margarita Maria, the young daughter of Philip IV of Spain and Queen Maria Anna. One of the maids is looking at the princess, but the princess herself is looking out 'at' us and so are some of the other people depicted. In particular, included in the scene is the painter himself, who stands with a palette and brush in his hands, facing a large canvas only the back of which is visible to us. The painter's look is towards us, hovering between his canvas and his subject—that subject being situated, logically, at the point where *we* stand. The looks of the painter and the princess, and others, seem to converge on the point from which we are ourselves looking. But, as we look, our eyes are drawn to the wall at the back of the room in the picture; that wall seems to be covered with pictures—then we realise that one of those 'pictures' is, after all, a mirror. And the mirror is so placed that we see a reflection in it, a reflection of two people apparently standing where we stand; the two figures in the mirror are also looking out at us, or back at themselves; they are the subject of the painter's look as he paints the canvas within the picture. There is, clearly, a kind of *vertigo* awaiting the spectator of this painting. The point at which the spectator stands is simultaneously the 'point' at which the painter stood for his own self-portrait in the painting and the point at which those two figures stand; if we see 'ourselves' in the mirror we also see the painter in the act of painting us, but we cannot see that portrait, only a self-portrait of the painter and a set of portraits of people looking at us being painted. The analysis could continue. One last point for now: the two figures visible in the mirror are, apparently, the royal parents, Philip IV and Queen Maria Anna—it is they whom we have replaced.

We can move from that to Jacques Lacan. One of the earliest and most fruitful notions that Lacan introduced into psychoanalysis is that of the 'mirror-phase'. Again, I will have to crudely summarise and simplify, as well as adapt. Lacan's essay on 'The mirror-stage as formative of the function of the 'I'' suggests the following: that the human infant is always born 'prematurely', in that birth occurs well before the motor-coordination of the body has occurred, whereas other animals at birth have already reached a far more advanced stage of their motor-coordination; the effect of this is that the infant's initial 'experience' is of a 'world' in which the distinction between 'self' and 'not-self' is not yet clear, the 'body' is experienced as amorphic, unstructured, without clear demarcation of its limits or 'internal' coherence—the infant is unable to bring into fixed location with each other its own limbs and bodily parts, its very surface is a mystery to it.

But when, at about the age of six months onwards, the infant first recognises its own reflection in a mirror, it sees 'itself' as a whole, a unit, complete and limited: its visible body is a coherent image, a symmetrical structure. The infant's response is worth noting: unlike, say, a cat faced with its own mirror-image, the human infant does not gaze fairly passively and quickly lose interest; it gesticulates, moves its arms, initiates a kind of *pas de deux* with its own reflection, discovers in movement the faithful accompaniment of its own body by the mirrored body; it thereby discovers its identification with that image to be reliable; indeed, in a stricter psychoanalytical sense the infant effects an 'identification, in the full sense that analysis gives to the term: namely, the transformation that takes place in the subject when he assumes an image' (Lacan).

Above all, this moment of playing with its own image is a jubilant moment for the infant: it acts with delight and fascination, with burbling pleasure. But the infant's recognition of itself has, in a certain sense, to be regarded as a mis-cognition, a mis-identification; there is a disparity, not least in the aspect of motor-coordination, between what the infant bodily *is* and what the infant sees itself *as*. And if we think of the infant as being held before the mirror by its mother, there is also a certain interaction of looks at work: the mother looks at the infant in the mirror and the infant in the mirror looks back at the mother looking; the infant before the mirror looks at itself looking at itself and at the mother looking at itself looking. Again, there is a certain vertigo of identifications implied in this interaction of looks.

At this point, let me introduce another notion drawn from Lacan's work which has been influential in film-criticism, the notion of 'suture'. In French, and in English, the word, as a verb, means to stitch the lips of a cut or wound after a surgical operation; the relevant sense of the word here is the sense of closing up a gap by intermittent joins, a gap that is made only to be healed up; the stitches hold in place two edges that will then fuse into a seam. In Lacan's use, particularly as articulated by J-A. Miller, the term has a very complex and technical application within psychoanalysis; but some film-theorists have adopted the term, in a rather simplifying way, to analyse what happens as we look at a film.

In particular, think of a conventional way of filming a dialogue between two people. First, we see person A as from person B's point of view, then we see B as from A's point of view—the 'shot/reverse-shot' pattern familiar in so many films. But in most instances of this shot/reverse-shot way of filming a dialogue, what we in fact see is A as from B's point of view, but not quite, since B's shoulder is often in the shot, visible in a lower corner of the frame: we are seeing A as if from over B's shoulder, slightly behind B rather than positioned exactly where B stands. But then, of course, when the reverse-shot is given us, not only are we now looking over A's shoulder at B, but there is nobody except B visible—just as in the first shot there was nobody visible looking over A's shoulder. The position, in spatial logic, from which 'we' look in either shot is shown, by the reverse-shot, to be empty, not occupied by any spectator. Clearly, the means by which this is achieved is simple: the camera is 'removed'. But the effect of apparently occupying this position of an *absent spectator* is curious: as spectators of the scene we are both there and not-there, we are both 'B seeing A' and 'A seeing B' but neither A nor B, yet we are not any visible 'C' either: we are both present and absent.

This fluctuation, or oscillation, of presence/absence is claimed to be at the source of our basic pleasure in watching a film; it is, so the argument or implication goes, a peculiarly pleasurable experience to be so situated that we are both present and absent, not simply in the sense in which having a 'cloak of invisibility' might allow us a certain voyeuristic satisfaction, but more basically in that our presence and absence are related to one another as a constant flickering or 'suturing' of presence/absence, a constant movement between the two positions, and the pleasure is derived from that constant loss of presence and regaining of presence, as if we were constantly in a situation of being annulled, cancelled out, annihilated, yet constantly overcoming that threat and re-establishing our continued presence, existence, being-there. It is this aspect of the whole case that the dialogue shot/reverse-shot pattern brings out so clearly, which is why it has sometimes been offered as a paradigm example of the process of watching a film.

Now, I'm actually rather dubious about the application of this notion in film-analysis, and particularly hesitant about any generalisation from the dialogue set-up to other aspects of film. But what I want to suggest is that the linking of pleasure to 'suture', to this oscillating presence/absence, is an important insight, and that it is in relation to the process of 'reading literature', rather than of watching a film, that this connection might be more clearly substantiated. To do so involves shifting our attention from 'looking' on to 'speaking', or what Plato would term 'mimicking'.

Take the following as an example—John Donne's 'The Flea':

Marke but this flea, and marke in this,
How little that which thou deny'st me is;
It suck'd me first, and now sucks thee,
And in this flea, our two bloods mingled bee;
Thou know'st that this cannot be said
A sinne, nor shame, nor losse of maidenhead,
    Yet this enjoyes before it wooe,
    And pamper'd swells with one blood made of two,
    And this, alas, is more than wee would doe.

Oh stay, three lives in one flea spare,
Where wee almost, yea more than maryed are,
This flea is you and I, and this
Our mariage bed, and mariage temple is;
Though parents grudge, and you, w'are met,
And cloysterd in these living walls of Jet.
    Though use make you apt to kill mee,
    Let not to that, seife murder added bee,
    And sacrilege, three sinnes in killing three.

Cruell and sodaine, hast thou since
Purpled thy naile, in blood of innocence?
Wherein could this flea guilty bee,
Except in that drop which it suckt from thee?
Yet thou triumph'st, and saist that thou
Find'st not thy seife, nor mee the weaker now;
    'Tis true, then learne how false, feares bee;
    Just so much honor, when thou yeeld'st to mee,
    Will wast, as this flea's death tooke life from thee.

Donne's poetry is, of course, often praised for the way it seems to capture the movement of speech: 'If it is a speaking voice that strikes us in the *Songs and Sonnets*, it is a voice with many inflexions and intonations . . ' (R. G. Cox). But it is, of course, *we* who have to *read* the poem with those shifting, constantly alive 'inflexions and intonations'. A 'good' reader of 'The Flea' will have to say the poem in a way that calls upon very subtle modulations of pace, tone, rhythm, etc.

But what happens as we try to read the poem in that way? If I'm reading the poem alone, in the privacy of my own room—which is the characteristic situation in which we read poetry, if at all, today—I find myself speaking the poem aloud, or at least *sotto voce*; I also find myself glancing up from the page, my look goes towards another point in the room that is, in a peculiar way, 'occupied' by a projected 'Other' to whom this poem is addressed ('and now sucks thee', 'Oh stay,'). That 'Other' is not, of course, 'present' in the room, yet saying the poem expressively, dramatically, 'with feeling', seems to demand another presence. Indeed, this poem demands of that Other that she should participate in the dramatic movement itself—between 'And this, alas, is more then wee would doe' and 'Oh stay, three lives in one flea spare' the action of the Other is clearly implied: she attempts to kill the flea—and my 'Oh stay' has to be said as a response to that imagined, projected act—just as 'Cruell and sodaine, hast thou since/Purpled thy naile, in blood of innocence', has to be in response to the Other's act of killing the flea. But there is no other person in the room, only a projected and invisible Other created by me as reader, as performer of the poem. It is not that I suffer hallucinations while speaking the poem, though my eyes might even take on precisely the expression they would have if someone were there! This Other has, indeed, a curious ontological status it might be worth exploring further. But at the moment it is the 'I' who is speaking that interests me more.

I find it difficult to read the poem, certainly aloud, without accompanying physical gestures, however minimal or re-strained and checked—a movement of the eyebrows, an angling of the head, a shrug of the shoulders. Yet, of course, these bodily 'reactions' (and the voice too is bodily) are not reactions to the 'Other', nor are they reactions to the 'text', inert marks on the page: they are constitutive of, part of, speaking (reading) the poem, and that is a controlled speaking, controlled in a peculiar sense. The 'words on the page' act, if you like, as a 'control' against which I measure my performance: my speaking those words in that order ('order' including punctuation marks, line-endings, etc.) is a kind of experiment, a testing out of ways of saying those words —I 'read' the poem in subtly or even markedly different ways each time.

One might even suggest that I am a bit like the infant before the mirror, *miming* to my own movements, mimicking and adjusting to the 'ideal' image (the aural image?) I envisage for this poem, bringing my vocal gestures into line with that ideal yet obliterating the 'ideal' in the process of pursuing it. The 'perfect' reading of this poem always eludes me; it too is like an Other whom I both respond to and simultaneously project. The poem is not so much a mirror held up to life as a mirror of and for my own Other.

Yet, at the same time, insofar as I operate the experiment, I am aware of my speaking as an experiment, a finding-out, a discovery of something I am not wholly responsible for; I control the 'I' who speaks, that 'I' too is an Other. Yet it is 'my' voice, my physical voice and gestures, that are at work in the speaking: it is still 'myself' that is being controlled. It seems to me that this peculiarly oscillating 'I', flickeringly present as both I and Other, is best understood along the lines suggested by Lacan's notion of 'suture'. It is as if 'I' were both present and absent, looking over my own shoulder rather than simply identified with myself, yet unable to be seen even in the mirror I hold up to myself. These are visual metaphors, and unsatisfactory. Yet they perhaps capture—by analogy with the pictorial and filmic examples I explored earlier—something of the 'vertigo' that seems to be involved as soon as one tries to analyse the process of speaking, mimicking, this poem.

It would be possible to explore this process in a more strictly Lacanian way. I will simply indicate what I mean by quoting Jacques-Alain Miller: 'Suture names the relation of the subject to the chain of its discourse.' In other words, the notion of suture would lead us into an understanding of the activity of speaking and writing more generally. I don't want, here, to develop that—partly because I don't have enough confidence in (my own grasp of) Lacan, and partly because I want to try to make clearer to myself some problems that I find I can't think about by simply taking over Lacan's approach and terminology. (It may also be that the kind of 'understanding' required can only be arrived at by and in a process of genuinely dialectical practice, though not necessarily by the style of process Lacan himself has adopted.)

Let me use Freud instead (if any Lacanians will excuse that 'instead'). In chapter II of *Beyond the Pleasure Principle*, Freud gives the famous account of his grandson's game of *Fort/Da*—how the eighteen-month-old infant played with his toys by throwing them out of sight and having them returned, these actions being marked by the child's utterance of '*Fort!*' ('Gone!') and '*Da!*' ('There!'). The account, and Freud's explanation in this chapter, are presumably familiar. I want to pick out a footnote, which reads:

> One day the child's mother had been away for several hours and on her return was met with the words 'Baby o-o-o-o!' which was at first incomprehensible. It soon turned out, however, that during this long period of solitude the child had found a method of making himself disappear. He had discovered his reflection in a full-length mirror which did not quite reach to the ground, so that by crouching down he could make his mirror-image 'gone'.

Clearly, this game gave the child a great deal of pleasure; Freud offers an account of why the game of *Fort/Da* with objects gave the child pleasure, but he doesn't actually comment on the pleasure to be derived from the mirror-version. It seems clear that what the child is doing is playing with his own disappearance in such a way as to control that disappearance, to manipulate it: repeatedly he makes 'himself' vanish in order to reappear; he deliberately oscillates between 'presence' and 'absence', and the point of the oscillation is to constantly re-affirm, re-establish, re-claim, his presence—not so much the repeated fact of his re-appearance, but the repeated act of re-appearing; the pleasure occurs not by being-present or by being-absent but by being in control of being-present and of being-absent (the one necessary to the other). It is the 'I' who is in control both of the present 'I' (in the mirror) and of the absent 'I' (invisible, not-looked-at) who is the delighted 'I'. This 'third I' is the creation of the game itself, a peculiar I not otherwise available or known; in the intermittent, jubilant delight of that 'I' the split between I and Other is recuperated, fused, healed over, sutured.

But the game is perhaps a fragile one, in two respects. First, the child remains visible throughout to others, remains 'there', does not 'actually' disappear; an adult can spoil the game by registering the continued visibility of the child crouched below the mirror; this mirror-version is essentially a private and 'better', but still vulnerable, version of the familiar adult-child game of 'I see!'—where the child is dependent upon the other continuing to call 'I see!' whenever the child chooses to re-appear. Secondly, and related to this, is the fact that it is 'only' the mirror-I who is under control, can be made to disappear; the ordinary I, this side of the mirror, remains, can only disappear from the mirror, not from the real room. Insofar as the child is still held within the identification of the mirror-phase this is perhaps an impossible distinction for the child fully to make—Lacan dates the mirror-phase from six to eighteen months, and Freud's grandson was eighteen months old. But such refinements can be left aside.

What I want to suggest is that the pleasure of reading 'The Flea' combines both the pleasure of the moment of the mirror-phase itself and the pleasure of the *Fort/Da* mirror-game. By the 'pleasure of reading' I mean not the particular pleasures of reading this poem, but the pleasure at work, or released, in the process of reading itself, why we get pleasure from this *kind* of reading. Let me label that reading-pleasure 'extasie'—in homage to Donne's poem 'The Extasie' which puts into play some allied notions. (Indeed, I am tempted towards conducting my argument almost entirely in terms of some of Donne's poems—'Witchcraft by a Picture', 'A Valediction: of my name, in the window', 'The Triple Foole'—but I'd better not.)

When I read 'The Flea' aloud I oscillate between speaking as 'I' and as 'Other' yet there is a kind of 'third I' who controls the fit or fusion between speaking I and speaking Other, 'measures' the one against the other, and uses as the norm for that measuring an 'ideal Other' whose voice would bear no trace of 'mine'; that ideal voice is perhaps experienced as a voice 'heard' but without physical embodiment, a voice audible only to the 'inner ear', the 'third ear', and my reading aloud of the poem may never measure up to that heard voice, though I try to mimic its subtleties, nuances, overtonal qualities, its many 'inflexions and intonations': *that* is the voice I hear in 'silent' reading.

What this process involves, then, is both a constant fluctuation in which I am absorbed by, dissolved in, taken over by, made absent by, an Other who takes my place, replaces me, speaks instead of me, yet never fully so, since I am also simultaneously in control of that oscillating presence/absence, shaping my voice in a flexibly 'mimicking' way, and yet never fully in control either, since any final fusion escapes me: the Other I produce is never quite the Other that I hear. It is this peculiar equilibrium between presence and absence which I maintain, this playing of control against subordination, this maintenance of self-presence at the edge of self-absorption, of evanescence, that provides the 'extasie' of reading: I am split into I and Other only to re-assert the unity of that I which allows the splitting.

Yet that unified I is itself under a double-demand, to maintain itself as intact, in control, over against the ideal Other and yet to reduce that ideal Other to the controlled Other who speaks in my voice. And in reading 'silently' I suppress the act of speaking aloud in order to effect an impossible fusion between the heard voice and the speaking I who does not speak, to identify the Other that I 'could' produce with the Other I hear—an attempted collapse of the actual into the ideal while preserving the insistence on the I who 'could' speak the perfect reading. But of course I could never speak aloud the voice I hear; while in silent reading the 'danger' of losing control, the threat of dissolution, is increased: 'I' fade into, am absorbed by, that heard Other I seek, im-mediately, to emulate: the reverse-shots no longer succeed each other but are superimposed.

It seems to me that it is this process which deeply underpins a dominant contemporary notion of 'literary value'. By that I mean that the possibility of such an oscillating and yet controlled, suturing, reading is felt to be a *sine qua non* for any claim of a text to being 'literature' at all, to having any value as 'literature' in the first place. What is deeply implicit in a certain tradition of criticism is the demand for that kind of 'extasie': unless a text can be read in that way, any further discussion of its particular qualities or 'value' is at best a reluctant discussion. Another, extreme but converging, way of putting that is to say that anyone who claimed that Donne's 'The Flea' was a 'good poem' because it could be used to seduce someone would be ruled out of court; what the literary critic is after isn't any particular *use* the poem might be put to, but a certain *frisson* to be got from *reading* it 'as a poem'. Or to put it another way, if a text can be read with (in) extasie, it can be discussed as 'literature'.

There are two sides to this coin of 'value'. The first is precisely that 'literary value' is to be sought as a 'pure' value, divorced (initially or in principle) from 'non-literary' considerations, to be discovered not in 'what' the text says but in 'the way it says it', which is then seen as controlling and creating 'what is said'; from there, the particular localisations of that 'way' can be explored, in terms of 'style', 'imagery', 'rhythm', 'tone' etc.—yet all these terms of analysis and comment are pointers to what is already 'known' to be there: 'literary value'; the details are a supportive spelling-out, not a demonstration or discovery (though they may be offered as such to someone else), and in most cases they can only be communicated to someone else not by formal argument or definition (what is 'tone'?) but by ostensive performance, by 'reading it *this* way'.

The obverse of this is that since it is the *reading* that provides the extasie, 'literary value' can be assigned to texts of very diverse kinds by different readers, and their subsequent disagreements are not to be resolved by simply pointing to this or that feature of the text but rather by a persuasion directed at changing the way the text is read, by, in effect, shaping the other's reading to place him or her within the process of suture, to 'experience it for themselves'. In this way, 'literary value' is a quality 'immediately recognisable' yet simultaneously utterly elusive.

Within critical discussion, a particular text may have (it's a partly frivolous point) a certain kind of exchange-value—compare this with that, the effect here is similar to the effect there, this does less successfully what that poem achieves, etc.—but there can be no unit of value nor can one text be substituted for another text (each is 'unique'), since finally it is not texts that are the objects of the literary critical exercise but rather the process of reading: what justifies the attention paid to a text is that someone 'values' it—i.e. has read it in an extatic way.

I'm aware that my case would have to be considerably elaborated in a number of directions and that I would have to meet a number of problems—not least those associated with a familiar kind of 'philosophy of literary criticism'. All I can do here is make some limited suggestions and sketch out four areas for further exploration.

First, it would be worth probing the way particular critics talk, when they do, about what it is they are doing, because I suspect that quite often the act of reading has an odd status in those accounts; to read in an extatic way seems both the premise, the prior condition, of any commentary and the final effect of any approving criticism, yet the actual process of reading is elided. (In specific 'practical criticism' or 'close reading' commentaries, the text is simply inserted, as quotation, into the analysis, with the assumption that it will be read in the way intended—a variation of this procedure is, of course, my own use of 'The Flea'; the difficulties this raises for 'close reading' of long novels are well-known.) Consider, as an example, this passage from Leavis, from his *Education and the University*:

> For surely, as one might say to one's beginning students, it should be possible, by cultivating attentive reading, to acquire a higher skill than the untrained reader has: a skill that will enable the trained reader to do more with a

poem than ejaculate approval or disapproval, or dismiss it with vaguely reported general impressions, qualified with the modest recognition that (in Arnold Bennett's words) 'taste after all is relative.' Analysis, one would go on, is the process by which we seek to attain a complete reading of the poem—a reading that approaches as nearly as possible to the perfect reading. There is about it nothing in the nature of 'murdering to dissect', and suggestions that it can be anything in the nature of laboratory-method misrepresent it entirely. We can have the poem only by an inner kind of possession; it is 'there' for analysis only in so far as we are responding appropriately to the words on the page. In pointing to them (and there is nothing else to point to) what we are doing is to bring into sharp focus, in turn, this, that and the other detail, juncture or relation in our total response; or (since 'sharp focus' may be a misleading account of the kind of attention sometimes required), what we are doing is to dwell with a deliberate, considering responsiveness on this, that or the other node or focal point in the complete organization that the poem is, in so far as we have it. Analysis is not a dissection of something that is already and passively there. What we call analysis is, of course, a constructive or creative process. It is a more deliberate following-through of that process of creation in response to the poet's words which reading is. It is a re-creation in which, by a considering attentiveness, we ensure a more than ordinary faithfulness and completeness.

What then, one might still ask, is the kind of 'attention' involved in an 'attentive reading'? Does 'reading' refer to an act of reading in the phrase 'a reading that approaches as nearly as possible to the perfect reading' (and whose is the 'perfect reading')? The last few sentences seem to oscillate between 'analysis' being a writing or talking about 'that process of creation in response to the poet's words which reading is' and analysis being ideally a way of actually reading the poem: 'It is a re-creation in which . . we ensure a more than ordinary faithfulness and completeness.' At the brink of this passage hovers a dissolving of reading into writing, a notion of writing as a mode of reading and vice-versa.

Second, there might well be an obverse side to the notion of reading as extasie; for a text to allow or prompt or demand such a reading it might have to have been written in a process akin to extasie: a kind of oscillating identification of the I who writes and the ideal projected or heard Other who speaks in the text but who is obliterated by the actual Other who is written. Only a detailed analysis could unpack this suggestion (the whole question of 'style' is involved) but such an analysis might easily begin from Plato's remarks about the poet 'seated on the Muses' tripod'. It would be interesting, for example, to compare the way in which Plato locates what I have called the 'ideal voice' as that of a god, with various modern accounts of literary creation in which the unconscious or the (impersonal) tradition are foregrounded.

Third, it is perhaps necessary to insist that my conclusion that the notion of 'literary value' (in the *sine qua non* sense) is rooted in a demand for an extatic reading is valid—if at all—within a particular history, of both 'literature' and 'criticism', and indeed within a history of the act of reading. The connections that would have to be explored are those between the emergence of our modern sense of 'literature' and 'the literary' some time between 1600 and 1800, the development of a particular mode of 'literary criticism' (in the nineteenth and twentieth centuries) tied to the 'experience' of 'literature', and the establishment of silent or solitary reading as the dominant habit of reading; the writings of John Donne and his contemporaries might figure in the account of all three aspects.

Yet while acknowledging the historical relativity of my argument, it has to be said that I, at least, find myself already situated within that history—my 'responses' to 'literature', my sense of what 'reading a poem' involves, my habits of reading, have been intimately shaped by that complex history; if I want to grasp the presuppositions and limitations of that history, that might best be done by an internal critique rather than by an external assault or a mere proffering of an alternative. The key process within that critical tradition has come to be the process of reading 'attentively', 'responsively'. By attending responsively to that process of attending responsively I have perhaps clarified, in a provisional way, why it is that the notion of 'literary value', which appears to be the defining notion at the heart of 'literary criticism', is something of a screen-notion, in the sense in which Freud uses 'screen-memory': the 'primal scene' of literature is always an act of a reader rather than a mysterious attribute of a text.

Fourth, there is a certain parallel between the notion of extatic reading and a Lacanian way of talking about 'love'. In Lacanian terms 'love' might be regarded as the desire for the desire of the Other. Put that another way: the following is a peculiarly Lacanian dialogue:

John: I, John, love you Jane
Jane: No, I, John, love you Jane
John: Yes, I Jane love you John.

We perhaps ought to take seriously one way of talking about 'literature' as involving a 'love'.

Now let me return, finally, to Marx, with three concluding pointers. First, I said earlier that Marx would look coldly on any attempt to somehow equate the notion of 'value' in his critique of political economy and the notion of 'value' in literary criticism. I also remarked that I thought that any attempt to push in the direction of Marx's question 'is value as such the general form, in opposition to use-value and exchange-value as particular forms of it?' would end in a *cul-de-sac*, in both political economy and literary criticism. But it is precisely because of that shared *cul-de-sac* that one can now suggest a certain equation between the use of 'value' in political economy and in literary criticism.

For it is clear that the footnote query I quoted from the *Grundrisse*, about 'value as such', was a side-track for Marx, leading him away from what could be regarded as the key break-through in his critique of political economy: the recognition that 'value as such' has no content as a concept and that any attempt to talk in terms of 'value as such' was fundamentally misleading. (Parenthetically, it's worth registering in this context the difficulty of clarifying even the notion of 'use-value' itself, and its converse 'need', in Marx.) One passage where the implications of this negative insight are clear enough is the following:

> Men do not . . bring the products of their labour into relation with each other as values because they see these objects merely as the material integuments of homogeneous human labour. The reverse is true: by equating their different products to each other in exchange as values, they equate their different kinds of labour as human labour. They do this without being aware of it. Value, therefore, does not have its description branded on its forehead; it rather transforms every product of labour into a social hieroglyphic. Later on, men try to decipher the hieroglyphic, to get behind the secret of their own social product: for the characteristic which objects of utility have of being values is as much men's social product as their language. The belated scientific discovery that the products of labour, in so far as they are values, are merely the material expressions of the human labour expended to produce them, marks an epoch in the history of mankind's development, but by no means banishes the semblance of objectivity possessed by the social characteristics of labour.

What Marx is pointing to here is that 'value' is not an attribute of an object but a form of relationship between social individuals, yet that fact is obscured for us precisely because we think of 'value' as somehow attached to things. Marx's own footnote to this passage captures the point succinctly:

> When Galiani said: 'Value is a relation between persons', he ought to have added: a relation concealed beneath a material shell.

47

That 'concealment' is what underpins the whole of the analysis in this section of *Capital*, on 'The Fetishism of the Commodity and Its Secret'. In a similar way, one could claim that to speak of 'literary value' is normally to commit oneself to a 'Fetishism of the Text', in the sense that 'value' is then seen as somehow an attribute of the 'work of literature', the text, rather than as indicating a 'relation between persons'. But whereas the 'persons' involved in the relation of commodity-exchange are 'a buyer' and 'a seller', two 'distinct' persons, the 'relation' at work in reading extatically is between what I have termed 'I', 'speaking I', 'speaking Other', 'third I' and 'ideal Other', and, sometimes, a further projected 'Other' (the addressed 'thee' of Donne's poem). These terms are clearly unsatisfactory, and this is partly because they tend to imply the presence (or presence/absence) of what we normally call 'persons'. And what we normally mean by 'person' is a unity of the 'I'. Of course, without that notion of the unified or fixed 'I' arguments about the somehow intrinsically one-sided capacities of people are much harder to sustain—a point that would take us right back to Marx's footnote on Plato's understanding of the 'division of labour', and could also lead us into considering the way in which reading and writing are a 'social product', a social 'labour', as 'language' itself is.

That also brings me to my second point. Insofar as extasie involves a vertigo of identifications, identities, projections, it calls into question the very notion of the 'unity' of the 'person' reading. To read Donne's 'The Flea' 'responsively', 'fully', 'appropriately' is to enter into a relationship with one's 'self' that challenges the very coherence of that 'self'; it is to create, in the process of reading, a palimpsest of 'I's and 'Others' in which the known, stable 'I' we normally identify with, identify ourselves as, is constantly effaced and lost; yet in the same movement, in a fluctuating and flickering way, that coherent I is re-established, re-asserts itself as the locus of control over the evanescence and vacillation. In subjecting my self to the reading I partially lose myself as subject, experience the 'I' of the reading as constituted by and in the act of reading. Much of the time, that stable, everyday I is dominant; in reading extatically it is possible to glimpse the dissolution of that everyday I, to become aware of that I as always constituted.

The grammar of the language does not, finally, allow an articulation of this dissolution, whatever the twists and turns of the offered formulations: inexorably, the language leads back to the subject. Yet it is possible to recognise that subject as a mis-cognition, and reading offers an accessible instance of that recognition. (Remember that Aristotle thought that writing might require someone 'with a touch of madness in him'.) Reading therefore has an ambivalent significance for any marxist critique of 'the subject': it both demonstrates or discloses the non-unity of the subject, opens onto the absence of the subject, yet also offers a constant recuperation of that unity: it is in reading that we can sometimes experience ourselves as most in control of ourselves as sources of meaning, originators of discourse: it is our reading, our emphases, tones, nuances, we offer; the poem means what we make it mean, take it to mean. Yet at the same time, in the same moment of speaking, we can seem most intimately obliterated, effaced, replaced by another voice which is not of our making but made by 'the poem itself'.

My third point is extremely tentative. In recent years, many attempts have been made to bring marxism, psychoanalysis, semiotics, literary criticism and film-theory into relation with each other. Often a hierarchy of relations has been postulated in which, in principle, marxism joins hands with psychoanalysis and both are brought to bear upon the literary or filmic text, thereby undercutting or replacing 'ideological' modes of criticism. It might now be useful to explore the self-contradictions involved in reading in order to grasp more clearly some of the concepts of both marxism and psychoanalysis, not least the marxist concept of ideology. That approach may risk a collapse back into discredited and discarded habits—of idealism, phenomen-ology, impressionistic vagueness, and, most heinous heresy of all, a lack of 'rigour'; it may be a return to ideology, but it may also promote an internal critique of ideology, a distanciation within ideology, an undermining of that subject which is not, finally, to be fully eradicated or exorcised.

Simply as a recapitulating coda, let me finally offer three interestingly inter-echoing quotations for you to read, one from Marx, one from Lacan, and one from T. S. Eliot:

In a certain sense, a man is in the same situation as a commodity. As he neither enters into the world in possession of a mirror, nor as a Fichtean philosopher who can say 'I am I', a man first sees and recognises himself in another man. Peter only relates to himself as a man through his relation to another man, Paul, in whom he recognises his likeness. With this, however, Paul also becomes from head to toe, in his physical form as Paul, the form of appearance of the species man for Peter.

Capital

For it is at the level at which subjective 'synthesis' confers its full meaning on speech that the subject reveals all the paradoxes of which he is the patient in this singular perception. These paradoxes already appear when it is the other who offers speech: this is sufficiently evidenced in the subject by the possibility of his obeying this speech in so far as it governs his hearing and his being-on-his-guard, for simply by entering the other's auditory field, the subject falls under the sway of a suggestion from which he can escape only by reducing the other to being no more than the spokesman of a discourse that is not his own or of an intention that he is holding in reserve.

But still more striking is the subject's relation to his own speech, in which the important factor is rather masked by the purely acoustic fact that he cannot speak without hearing himself. Nor is there anything special about the fact that he cannot listen to himself without being divided as far as the consciousness is concerned. Clinicians did better by discovering verbal motor hallucination by detecting the outline of phonatory movements. Yet they have not articulated where the crucial point resides; it is that the sensorium being indifferent in the production of a signifying chain:

(a) this signifying chain imposes itself, by itself, on the subject in its vocal dimension

(b) . . . .

(c) its own structure *qua* signifier is determinant in this attribution, which, as a rule, is distributive, that is to say, possesses several voices, and, therefore, renders equivocal a supposedly unifying percipient.

'On the possible treatment of psychosis'

The point of view which I am struggling to attack is perhaps related to the metaphysical theory of the substantial unity of the soul: for my meaning is, that the poet has, not a 'personality' to express, but a particular medium, which is only a medium and not a personality, in which impressions and experiences combine in peculiar and unexpected ways . . . .

This essay proposes to halt at the frontier of metaphysics or mysticism, and confine itself to such practical conclusions as can be applied by the responsible person interested in poetry.

'Tradition and the Individual Talent'

*

ENCLAVES AND CUL-DE-SACS?

Literary criticism seems to be in an odd *cul-de-sac* at present. Two recent works by widely-esteemed critics can serve as pointers to a persistent paradox.* In reviewing together works by Barbara Hardy and Raymond Williams I don't intend to do 'justice' to each volume individually, but to suggest, by their juxtaposition, a curious state of affairs: the simultaneous importance and irrelevance of 'literature'—its importance within an educational apparatus and as the focus of a political project, and yet a concomitant sense that neither critic, or approach, has much to say about why anyone might actually continue reading poems and novels anyway. As a link, or diversion, I also glance at an aspect of Walter Benjamin's work still largely unappreciated—his criticism of Brecht's poems.

Barbara Hardy entitles her book *The Advantage of Lyric: Essays on Feeling in Poetry*. Almost every word here invites comment, but the most provocative is 'advantage'. The 'advantage of lyric in itself is its concentrated and patterned expression of feeling. This advantage is negatively definable: the lyric does not provide an explanation, judgment or narrative; what it does provide is feeling, alone and without histories or characters.' (p. l). The absence of history and explanation is frequently noted, and approved; an interesting example is the quoting (p. 5) of Quiller-Couch's cut-down version of Emily Bronte's long poem *Julian M. and A. G. Rochelle*: in Q's version 'virtually all we are left with is the intense lyrical

---

* Written 1977. Books discussed are Barbara Hardy, *The Advantage of Lyric*, The Athlone Press, 1977, pp. 142, £5.50. R. Williams, *Marxism and Literature*, Oxford University Press, 1977, pp. 218 £3.50. W. Benjamin, *Understanding Brecht*, New Left Books, 1973, which includes 'From the Brecht Commentary' and 'Commentaries on Poems by Brecht'. The general argument of this article might be taken further and modified by considering also Terry Eagleton's *Criticism and Ideology*, NLB, 1976, and Gabriel Josipovici's *The Lessons of Modernism*, Macmillan, 1977.

evocation of Hope' and this turns a narrative of tyranny and physical imprisonment into a lyric of 'spirit tormented by flesh' (p. 6). Specific response becomes transmuted into metaphysical universality. An alternative title for the poem is *The Prisoner. A Fragment.* As a fragment, it tempts us tantalisingly, like tourists contemplating a name scratched on an ancient dungeon wall: we respond to the imagined personal agony and forget the complex historical determinants of any specific imprisonment. As in the lyrics of the trench-poets, a whole war may be received, inadequately, in the form of private suffering. But Hardy apparently sees only the advantage not the disadvantages of this reducing perspective.

The structure of her book enacts a similar reduction. Each chapter focuses on a particular poet, ranging from John Donne to Sylvia Plath, and though occasionally a gesture is made towards biography or history, these poets are presented throughout as collections of poems, words on pages, largely without 'histories or characters'. The focus is on the poems 'themselves' ('lyric in itself') but it is then an unstable and oscillating focus. Some individual poems receive detailed explication, others are glanced at, others merely pointed at in passing. This raises problems for the reader: one never knows quite whether the phrase 'in another poem' presages a two-line précis, a casual comparison of a specific aspect, a page-length exegesis, or a Pevsnerian *bon mot*; so reading Hardy becomes a jittery business, one's finger constantly poised over the index to the relevant *Collected Poems*. But to what purpose?

Each chapter does have a kind of thesis—that Auden's poetry is reticently revealing, that Plath's offers us 'enlargement' rather than 'derangement'—but then what is it that we are learning? A particular poem may enact a reticent emotion, and a number of poems written by Auden may do so; but other poems written by other poets may also do so, and each does so in its own way. In writing a chapter on 'The Reticence of W.H. Auden' or on 'Clough's Self-Consciousness', is Hardy offering us covert character-psychology, after all; but wouldn't that invite consideration of other factors than the words on the page (e.g. the English upper-class code of emotional reticence? inter-war reticence about specifically homo-sexual affection? etc.)? This grouping of poems under the aegis of single authors and the uneven distribution of precision, the shifting proportion of commentary to text, point beyond Hardy's own book to more general problems.

At one point Hardy remarks (p. 63): 'I need not labour the local dramatisations of feeling' in some lines of Hopkins. Too true. For most of the readers she can expect will have already learned to practise the kind of practical criticism and close reading she provides; we are all inheritors of the Richards-Eliot-Empson-Leavis approach. And, despite some fine demonstrations of Hardy's skill in this familiar mode, there is a constant sense of either over-elaboration or under-analysis: if one line of quotation generates ten lines of exploration and unpacking, we can feel bombarded with the unnecessary; but if a ten-line poem is pinned down in a critical phrase, we feel free to dissent from the too-swift judgment.

The problem lies not so much in any individual imbalance of apportionment but in a general inheritance and transmutation. To establish an approach, or way of reading, was an achievement, a paradigm shift that necessitated a full account of the crucial experiment (one thinks of Leavis's 'Notes in the Analysis of Poetry'), but then the 'ordinary'. practitioner can seem a mere repetition of the master, a marginal and even superfluous voice. Moreover, if the origins of 'close reading' lie in the face-to-face teaching-situation ("This is so—isn't it?") its transmutation into the monologue of print is radically disabling: at the point of dissent or query, further persuasion is unforthcoming, the critic is silent where we seek to test her, garrulous where we already agree. And since *performance* (of the tone, the rhythm, the crucial emphasis) is a part of critical persuasion, the printed text is a clumsy medium for the gesture of conversion: either we read the poem like *that* already or we remain unsure that we have heard the critic's variant reading as it's intended.

This problem looms largest in basic disagreements. If the (second) 'advantage' of the lyric is that 'it creates and discovers feeling under the guise of affirming it, and does not have to discuss, analyse, explain or imitate it' (p. 2), the critic in discussing, analysing and explaining that feeling cannot convince us of its 'value' unless she can also create that feeling in our reading of the poem. But that way eloquence lies. And in disagreeing with critical colleagues Hardy is sometimes reduced to an indignant eloquence: 'I would like to disagree with this in the strongest possible terms and insist that Clough's poetry is strongly sensuous both in music and in visual imagery'—thus begins an eight-page attempted demolition of Walter Houghton's contrary opinion. But the insistence is mainly assertion: 'Clough never writes coldly, dryly or cynically' (p. 45). Never? But what if I read him dryly or cynically; isn't coldness a matter, in part, of spoken tone? One can analyse verbal complexity or demonstrate technical virtuosity, but can the printed word enforce a particular performance of 'feeling'? If it could, the poet would not require his commentator.

But why does he require that commentator anyway? More to the point, why do we require either poet or commentator? Hardy's disagreement with Houghton is instructive. It is a tactic of professionalism, or twitch of scholarship, like some of the footnotes: 'She is also Grania, as her Adonis is Dermid. Yeats may even be echoing or remembering Samuel Ferguson's poem 'The Death of Dermid', *Lays of the Western Gael*, 1865 . . . ' (p. 79n). The essay on Clough was first published in *The Major Victorian Poets: Reconsiderations*, the chapter on Yeats in *Modernist Studies*, volume 1, No 2, 1974. The 'Acknowledgements' show that the whole book has been previously published, each chapter as a contribution to a periodical or symposium. Presumably the book itself will find a niche somewhere in the same libraries that house those periodicals and symposia, and hundreds like them, and thousands of books like this one.

Hardy herself quotes what she calls 'an affectionate conceit' from Auden's *Homage to Clio*:

> I dare not ask if you bless the poets
> For you do not look as if you ever read them
> Nor can I see a reason why you should.

The tone of course is crucial. But why should we? What is the 'advantage of lyric' and over what? The 'should' of Auden's line rather uneasily takes on a different but familiar echo: "You should read Barbara Hardy's analysis of Auden's reticence—you'll find it in *The Review* Nos. 11/12, 1964." It's the tone of the don to the conscientious student of Literature, writing his essay on Auden's middle period. That, perhaps, is the major transmutation of our literary inheritance—and a set of essays on individual poets ("Next week we're doing Z"), published with a title that suggests a genre ("I'm taking the Lyric course this term."), under the imprint of the University of London Athlone Press at £5.50 for 140 pages, slots neatly into it.

To read a poem with one's index finger pinioned elsewhere in the volume, ready to flick to another poem, to 'compare and contrast', is a curious but characteristic activity of the critic. But even if we focus on the individual poem, we may well respond to its 'concentrated and patterned expression of feeling' —only to find ourselves expressing our feeling for its concentrated pattern: which is not the same thing at all. The subtlest traps and temptations lurk here. For in taking the lyric as the quintessential literary form (apparent in the endeavour to read novels and plays as dramatic poems), the post-Eliot critics may have helped to create the conditions for the apparent irrelevance of poetry for most of us today. We learned to read literary works as 'objective correlatives' of feelings, but those feelings were present to us only *in* the work, a 'new *art* emotion' (Eliot's phrase in 'Tradition and the Individual Talent'): the work thereby became an objective correlative—of itself. From the position that 'It is not in his personal emotions, the emotions provoked by particular events in his life, that the poet is in any way remarkable or interesting', it was dangerously easy to move to the notion that reading a poem (still more, the 'reading' of a poem) need not be 'provoked by particular events' in our own lives or have any specific relation to them: the feelings we were invited to discover 'in poetry' (cf. 'Essays on Feeling *in* Poetry') were to be also divorced from our own 'histories or characters'—but that meant that reading poetry could be only a (higher?) form of leisure amusement or an academic exercise.

We could then invite and expect students to read love-poems, war-poems, or nature-poems not for what they might (want to) discover about love, war, or nature, nor for what they might (want to) discover about Donne, Owen, Edward Thomas or themselves as lovers or fighters, but for what they might (be obliged to) say about 'Thinking and Feeling in the Songs and Sonnets of John Donne' (chapter 2) or 'Passion and Contemplation in Yeats's Love Poetry' (chapter 5). But then, of course, they might be better advised to read, instead, the critics who had written about such curious topics (if they—or the library—could afford the relevant books). And if the poems themselves happened to provoke a desire to make love, make war, or go for a walk, that had nothing to do with responding appropriately to the '*art* emotion' *in* the poem—which was their proper concern. And it could always be intimated to anyone else (a historian, an engineer, a housewife, a computer programmer) who ventured to respond to a poem that, really, 'poems' weren't *their* proper concern either. A curious circle had closed, with only the literary critic on the inside. Barbara Hardy's book is very much the work of an insider and in its intermittent struggles to escape its own origins it mainly demonstrates the tenacity of their hold.

The deadening grip can be broken, at some cost. In his 'Commentaries on Poems by Brecht', Walter Benjamin wrote:

> It is a known fact that a commentary is something different from a carefully weighed appreciation apportioning light and shade. The commentary proceeds from the classic nature of its text and hence, as it were, from a pre-judgement . . The difficulty to be surmounted here consists in reading lyric poetry today at all . . corresponding exactly to . . the difficulty of writing

lyric poetry today . . It is the commentary's purpose to pinpoint the political contents of passages chosen precisely because they are purely lyrical.

And in speaking of Brecht's poems as 'attempts to make gestures quotable', those gestures evincing 'not what a man is convinced of . . but what his convictions make of him', Benjamin notes:

> These words, like gestures, must be practised, which is to say first noticed and later understood. They have their pedagogical effect first, their political effect second, and their poetic effect last of all. The purpose of the commentary . . is to advance the pedagogical effect as much as possible and to retard the poetic one.

What 'pedagogical' means here might be indicated by one sentence: 'The *Handbook for City Dwellers* provides object lessons in underground activity and emigration.' And Benjamin, himself also in exile, rightly pinpoints the precise historical-biographical moment for these lessons:

> For the intelligent Communist, the final five years of his political work in the Weimar Republic signified a crypto-emigration. Brecht experienced these years as such. This may have provided the immediate occasion for the writing of this cycle of poems. Crypto-emigration was a preliminary form of actual emigration; it was also a preliminary form of underground political activity.

But in moving from objective correlatives to object lessons, from vicarious feelings to quotable gestures, from the exclusion of historical explanations to the analysis of historical possibilities, the critic again faces traps and temptations—those of an easy equation between political commitment and literary quality, or dogmatic demands for specific literary practices and options. Stemming from those dilemmas there has been a long debate about the politics of literary criticism and specifically about the relationship between 'marxism' and 'literary criticism'.

In England, the work of Raymond Williams has been one local focus for that debate. His new book is boldly, simply and ambitiously entitled *Marxism and Literature.* The title already indicates a problem. Consider those echoed titles of Williams's earlier books, *Reading and Criticism*, *Culture and Society*, *The Country and the City*: the 'and' in these titles suggests a tension but also an overlap, a completion by interpenetration or mutual supplementation, a gesture towards possible wholeness. The other strain in Williams's titles suggests a movement, a process, a probable incompletion: *Drama from Ibsen to Brecht*, *The English Novel from Dickens to Lawrence*, *Long Revolution.* But the new title seems merely an inert juxtaposition, a rather wary bringing together of two terms that operate in different lexical worlds (not even a provocative gesture like *Modem Tragedy*, or *Keywords*, more like the statement of a problem, as in *Television: Technology and Cultural Form*). The new book is actually one in a series of 'Marxism and ——' titles, but—the thought arises—might it not equally be one in a series of '—ism and Literature' titles (Buddhism and Literature, Catholicism and Literature, Fascism and Literature)? Characteristically, Williams anticipates the thought:

> Even twenty years ago, and especially in the English-speaking countries, it would have been possible to assume, on the one hand, that Marxism is a settled body of theory or doctrine, and, on the other hand, that Literature is a settled body of work, or kinds of work, with known general qualities and properties. A book of this kind might then reasonably have explored problems of the relations between them or, assuming a certain relationship, passed quickly to specific applications. The situation is now very different.

But then, equally characteristically, Williams offers himself as the third term, linking the other two; he traces his own 'relation to Marxism and to literature which, between them, in practice as much as in theory, have preoccupied most of my working life'. The reading eye hesitates, and goes back. Williams's commitment to 'Socialism' has been an open secret, but that is not the same as a preoccupation with Marxism (at least in England, over a long period), and Williams's own relations with Marxism as a body of theory have only fairly recently been a matter of public explicitness. One's hesitation persists as one reads: Williams speaks of his work over thirty-five years as 'in direct if often unrecorded contact, throughout, with Marxist ideas and arguments', and of his present position as a 'new and conscious relation with Marxism', his present theory as 'in my view, a Marxist theory'.

Insofar as Williams's work over the years has represented, for many followers, a paradigm-shift, replacing and supplanting Leavis, he is right to suggest, modestly, that his 'individual history may be of some significance in relation to the development of Marxism and of thinking about Marxism in Britain'; the question then raised by these more explicit declarations might be whether the new book signals an epistemological break in Williams's own thinking. But to speak of an 'epistemological break' may be to speak as the kind of 'Marxist' Williams now sees himself as having once been, from 1939 to 41: 'it can mean that a style of thought and certain defining propositions are picked up and applied, in good faith, as part of a political commitment, without necessarily having much independent substance'.

These apparently preliminary remarks by Williams go, in one sense, to the heart of the book. For its main target is the practice of taking terms of analysis for terms of substance. One formulation can stand for many:

> the analytical categories, as so often in idealist thought, have, almost unnoticed, become substantive descriptions, which then take habitual priority over the whole social process to which, as analytical categories, they are attempting to speak.

It is presumably not an accident, but a tactic, that Williams shows very particularly how linguistics, in its development from classical studies through nineteenth-century comparative philology to Saussure and beyond, has adopted a notion of language as a fixed, objective, and in these senses 'given' system, which had theoretical and practical priority over what were described as 'utterances' (later as 'performance'). Thus the living speech of human beings in their specific social relationships was theoretically reduced to instances and examples of a system which lay beyond them.

Variations of this reversal are traced. Within the study of language itself, the 'referential' and the 'emotive', the 'denotative' / 'connotative' and 'ordinary' / 'literary' language distinctions came to act not as categories of analysis but as names for demarcated areas of language. In Marxist theory, 'base' and 'superstructure' came to indicate rigidly separated entities (whatever their dialectical relationships thereafter). In literary criticism, 'genre' assumed almost an independent existence, 'prior' to individual works. Williams's tactic against these hypostasised usages is to track their histories, recover their complex pedigrees, and in these frequent analyses of word-traces we hear most clearly the echoes and accents of earlier work—*Culture and Society* and *Keywords*. Interwoven with this strand are other echoes and repetitions of themes from earlier works: 'dominant, residual and emergent' and 'structures of feeling' are now titles of individual chapters, no longer phrases that play through other analyses but now the objects of analysis and quasi-definition themselves.

Most of this new book therefore induces a distinct sense of *déja-vu* for anyone who has followed Williams's previous work. What we seem to be offered is a shuffling of familiar pieces, an ordering of parts into a fairly predictable pattern. That pattern has its interest, of course; it becomes an intriguing question as to which theme or emphasis will link up next, as 'Base and Superstructure' leads to 'Determination' then to 'Productive Forces', 'Reflection and Mediation', 'Typification and Homology', 'Hegemony', etc. And one notes, with the pleasure of recognition, where those remembered comments on Lukacs or Goldmann or Gramsci find their new place. In one sense, therefore, the new book offers a summary and summation of most of Williams's already published work—and as such is both too complex to further summarise here and, presumably, too familiar to require it.

But then the question arises as to how one receives, and judges, this summation. One approach to an answer lies in the significance of the many excursions into the history of key-words and of debates. What purpose do they serve in the text itself? One might see them as variations on a Cartesian circle: Williams himself speaks of a 'radical doubt', 'when the most basic concepts —the concepts, as it is said, from which we begin—are suddenly seen to be not concepts but problems, not analytical problems either but historical move-ments that are still unresolved.' But how can one begin to speak when the only terms available are themselves the problems? At times this dilemma can seem like a variant on an older idealist epistemological problem. Or one might see Williams as practising in these word-histories his own form of Whiggery: he presents an interpretation of others' positions so that they culminate, inescapably, in his own. Thus, after labelling his own current position 'cultural materialism', he can say of Marx's achievement: 'the stress on material history . . . was in one special way compromised. Instead of making cultural history material, which was the next radical move, it was made dependent, secondary, superstructural.' Others' positions become, similarly, 'not material enough' compared with Williams's own 'materialist' stance. But in either of these modes, Cartesian or Whiggish, these mini-histories of terms and positions would have to be seen as merely sleight-of-hand, a tactic or twitch of scholarship, since Williams's own eventual formulations and theories would in any case have to stand, finally, on their own merits, whatever the difficulty of a starting-point or their relation to others' positions.

But a more positive way of understanding these backward glances is to turn this last comment on its head and in so doing to grasp the word-histories as exemplifying the central and, to some extent, new positive thesis of the book. Against the structuralist-linguistics emphasis Williams now offers Volosinov and Vygotsky. The basic notion here is that of the 'multi-accentual' character of all language in practical use; since we always use language within a social, interactional situation, language is always a matter of differential emphasis, not merely in, say, pronunciation, but, crucially, in meaning. The relation between 'form' and 'meaning' within the 'sign' is not fixed (as notions of system or code tend to make it) but flexible, within an active social relationship between living people. We each, if you like, bend the language we speak our own way. And this is precisely what we see Williams himself doing: his interlocutors are previous theorists; he takes their terms and bends them to his own voice and meaning. The typography is the material index of this process: a particular term may appear as, say, 'material', *material* or, simply, material (without either inverted commas or italics); with the first it operates as someone else's usage; italicised, it registers Williams's modified emphasis; and it then takes its unremarked place as meaning something new. It's an often successful device: we do indeed find ourselves moving, as we read, across a range of meanings, beginning to read with Williams's own unique accentuation.

But, oddly, we can then see how this tactic unites the ploys of both idealist epistemology and Whiggish historiography. The first parallel is with Aristotle. In surveying the theories of his predecessors concerning a topic, Aristotle characteristically offers himself as the synthesis and does so by proposing a terminology; necessarily, that terminology is drawn either from those prede-cessors themselves or, by metaphor, from other fields of usage. Thus, he can 'solve' the problem of the One and the Many and Parmenides's paradox of becoming and being, by speaking of 'potency' and 'act'; but do these terms solve or merely dissolve the problem? Since, however, they are the 'concepts from which we begin', we cannot now think (metaphysically) beyond or without them. Yet Aristotle's initiating privilege cannot be repeated. Hegel perhaps tried, in his own Whiggish/Idealist blend of historiographical epistemology, to begin anew. But whereas at least some of Aristotle's terms remained inescapable common sense until Heidegger, Hegel's system seemed radically ambiguous even to his immediate disciples. The split into Left and Right Young Hegelians was crucially a matter of political interpretation of a densely ambivalent style of writing.

Consider now the case of Williams. He writes, for example: 'A Marxism without some concept of determination is in effect worthless.' He then surveys both Marx's various German terms and a range of English usages—for example, 'determination' of a calculation, a course of study, a lease, as setting bounds or limits, as external determinism, as determined laws. This section concludes:

> This is where the full concept of determination is crucial. For in practice determination is never only the setting of limits; it is also the exertion of pressures. As it happens, this is also a sense of 'determine' in English: to determine or be determined to do something is an act of will or purpose.

This then allows Williams to achieve the required synthesis:

> Determination of this whole kind—a complex and interrelated process of limits and pressures—is in the whole social process itself and nowhere else: not in an abstracted 'mode of production' nor in an abstracted 'psychology'.

But then this 'full concept' leaves all the political options open, in practice; the term 'determination' can receive equally the accentuation of a Stalin, a Sorel, or a Situationist.

That, Williams might say, is precisely what he intends. It is a constant emphasis of the book that 'situations, relationships and responses' are always 'varying and *in principle* variable' (his emphasis). Allied to this formulation is another, italicised throughout by Williams:

> no mode of production and therefore no dominant social order and therefore no dominant culture ever in reality includes or exhausts all human practice, human energy, and human intention.

64

But then if we ask what is 'in reality' excluded in a particular case, the theoretical response can only be: 'It is an open question: that is to say, a set of specific historical questions'.

This emphasis, against others, may be salutary; but then do all historical (and philosophical?) questions become 'open questions' as all political options are 'open options'. When Williams says, of his discussion of 'commitment', that 'these qualifications are not meant to weaken the original claim, but simply to clarify it', we can sense the unease; but when he goes on to say that 'Alignment in this sense is no more than a recognition of specific men in specific (and in Marxist terms, class) relations to specific situations and experiences', the parenthesis is hardly a clarification of a formulation which has now weakened from a polemical proposition into a toothless tautology. And it is then noticeable that 'class' is the one term that Williams nowhere in his book seeks to examine or define afresh—or even to dissolve. A Marxism without a specifiable historical method and without a specifiable political practice, but which still speaks in a 'class' accent, may not cease to be entitled 'Marxist'; but it may then be merely a matter of terminology, a category of analysis and not a matter of substance, whether we call that position 'Marxist' or not.

Whether we call a particular piece of writing 'Literature' or not may also be an open question. It has certainly had a historically variable answer, as Williams usefully shows in chapter 3. The emphasis of his final chapter, 'Creative Practice', is—refreshingly—on the creative character of all writing, as 'always in some sense self-composition and social composition'. But if we ask why we might read what is now, more narrowly, known as 'Literature' Williams again appears synthetically evasive. He writes: 'Works of art, by their substantial and general character, are often especially important as sources of this complex evidence' for a 'cultural analysis' of the 'hegemonic in its active and formative but also its transformational processes'. On the same page he also writes:

The finite but significant openness of many works of art, as signifying forms making possible but also requiring persistent and variable signifying responses, is then especially relevant.

The second formulation might lead to an articulation of why reading literature might be not only a matter of 'evidence'—as, say, listening to the *Archduke Trio* is not only a matter of hearing evidence about the declining role of Archdukes in the Habsburg Empire. But Williams has little to say in this direction. He is right to protest that

> it is still difficult . . to prevent any attempt at literary theory from being turned, almost *a priori*, into critical theory, as if the only major questions about literary production were variations on the question 'how do we judge?

and he is right to remark that 'genre-classification . . can indeed be left to academic and formalist studies'. But to leave literature as either 'evidence', in however complex a form, or as an object for genre-classification, is perhaps still to leave open the most difficult question of all in this area: why we should read (let alone 'bless') the poets in the first place.

In *Marxism and Literature* Williams has perhaps tried to achieve a magisterial position and tone, a bending of a massively complex debate towards a resolution that transcends current polemical standpoints. For his own 'struggle at the roots of the mind', here as elsewhere, he deserves and earns much more than respect. But the resolution he offers may be only a matter of sustained resolve, his solutions only verging on the brink of dissolution, his synthesis only a matter, finally, of proposing 'terms of analysis as terms of substance'. But, to adapt yet another formulation from his own book,

> this specific solution is never mere flux. It is a structured formation which, because it is at the very edge of semantic availability, has many of the characteristics of a

pre-formation, until specific articulations—new semantic figures—are discovered in material practice.

Perhaps, however, until such 'new semantic figures' are made, in practice, aspiring critics and writers of this generation, 'Marxist' or otherwise, may still be left pondering bleakly those lines from Auden's *Homage to Clio*—and applying them ruefully to themselves:

> I dare not ask if you bless the poets
> For you do not look as if you ever read them
> Nor can I see a reason why you should.

*

POSTMODERNISM, LITERARY PRODUCTION
AND MULTIMEDIA

Competing mappings abound, of course. Postmodernism can be claimed as 'post' that Modernism evoked by a generation of grand names, artists, authors, architects: say, 1910-1940: Eliot, Joyce, Proust, Braque, Leger, Le Corbusier —candidates can be quarrelled over. Or as the *cadenza* concluding that hope of Modernisation once dated to the several industrial revolutions of England, France, Germany, and proleptically extended to the second or third world, the fourth planet, or utopia itself —the kickstart variously seen as a spinning jenny, Adam Smith, or Friedrich Hegel. Or, in epochal or apocalyptic mood, as whatever rough beast now presides over the closing tremors of a Modernity that stretched from 1450 to 1950, from Gutenberg and Copernicus to Hitler or Hiroshima. And, of course, postmodernists can in any case coyly eschew all such periodising placements, refuse historical linearities and sequencings, claim the perennial privilege of irruption into any tidy timeline.

Definitions are not worth disputing. What remains intriguing is why in the few decades during which the term 'postmodernism' proliferated, such ambiguities and unresolved hetereogeneities of reference and chronological implication could have so publicly co-existed in such continuing confusion and unclarity. What was it (is it?) about these decades that promoted such a hopelessly entangled term to such prominence? It has surely been an odd kind of vogue that has been unable to decide whether it finalises fifty years, one hundred and fifty, or five hundred. Or is that a clue to the very character of 'postmodernism'?

We can begin from the narrowest of postmodernist claims, restricting our initial inquiry to that specific inflection and single domain, of postmodernism as indicating a literature, a writing practice, somehow subsequent to the High

Modernism of Eliot's generation. Some immediate hesitancies and indeterminacies surface: that the term 'Modernism' is itself unstable, able retrospectively to embrace Flaubert or Baudelaire, or be assimilated back into Romanticism or Realism, as respectively the modernising breakthroughs of sensibility or of the city, or perhaps even as stretching back all the way from Mallarmé to Montaigne, an epochal undercurrent already contesting postmodernism's putative retrospective territorial claims. The notorious plasticity of literary history allies here with the all-embracing appetite of some (post)modernist critics for appropriating miscellaneous selected precursors as foreshadowing features of the (post)modern. It is, however, pointless to scrutinize these several variations without a wider framework to encompass them.

A playful hypothesis, therefore, a metaphor or shorthand not to be taken with any rigour: think of the very term 'literature' as itself subject to sliding redefinition according to a simple formula (remotely akin to a Mandelbrot set or fractal iteration):

$$a^2 + a = b$$
$$b^2 + a = c \text{ and so on.}$$

Viz, take a number and square it, add the original number; the result is further squared, and the original number again added; that sum is then squared and the original number added once more, and so on. In the process the weight of the originating number within the successive totals rapidly diminishes ($2^2 + 2 = 6$; $6^2 + 2 = 38$; $38^2 + 2 = 1446$).

Now substitute for the original number some form of linguistic performance or utterance, a language event occurring within a social practice, itself perhaps constitutive of a social apparatus: a declaration of love, a prayer to the almighty, a defence speech. One way of generating the 'literary' is by taking such a language event and in one or several ways 'squaring' it, while also retaining the original utterance-function within the resulting composite or composition. The term 'squaring' here merely indicates any form of reflexive re-working or feed-back operation which turns some element of the original performance into a feature with its own significance or interest, over and above its contribution to the original language event.

Calligraphy offers one kind of instance. The shape of the letters are accorded an exact attention, the hand trained towards skilful precision or flourish; the handwriting remains a legible inscription but its features are foregrounded as more than just the writing of a hand concerned to communicate. In Islamic tradition such skill could earn its practitioner fabulous wealth. My normal execrable scribble strives to communicate or express some content, but when I concentrate on perfecting the visible character of my letter formation according to some criterion of pleasing art, the communicative function remains but is perhaps even obscured or rendered less legible by the calligraphic elaboration. I may now, of course, take that calligraphic script and further rework it [$b^2 + a = c$] into, say, an elaborate pattern to decorate a mosque dome, though the original content may still remain decipherable through the second iteration.

This general formula is open to several kinds of implementation. Celtic illumination may so elaborate the underlying script towards labyrinthine interweaving as to leave only a patterned illegibility. In cabbalistic or numerological exercises the mathematical aspects of writing, however arbitrarily defined, may be foregrounded. Georges Perec's attempt to compose a novel without the letter 'e' or Hugo Ball's valiant sound poems exhibit other applications of the formula. Less idiosyncratically, George Herbert's *The Temple* incorporates several iterations: a prayer given verse form but also visibly organised as a diagrammatic emblem, while remaining eminently prayable. The final sequences in Aeschylus's *Oresteia* trilogy present prosecution and defence speeches versified and dramatised while remaining exemplary of a legal resolution, the whole contest itself subject to demo-cratic audience judgement. Mere mundane correspondence can be variously reworked as a verse epistle (Pope), an epistolatory novel (Richardson), a public intervention (Junius) or a philosophical post-card (Derrida). On this scale *The Waste Land* might be somewhere around e^2 and *Finnegans Wake* rapidly approaching the condition of y^2.

This way of formulating the 'literary' might be compared or counterposed to more familiar notions of formalism, but the formula is offered only as a shorthand notation through which to suggest a further argument. If 'literature' occurs where some such operation as $[a^2 + a = b]$ obtains, then obviously the composite result [b] can itself become a language event within another apparatus: the institution of Literature. Several reworkings of 'literary history' might thus be sketched, for example the tendency towards occluding or ignoring all links with any originating social practice (a tendency known as aesthetics), or conversely the problematic extrapolation back to some hypothetical actuality from a literary elaboration ('Courtly Love' might be such a case), though it would be an odd kind of category mistake to describe as a love poem a composition utterly unable to be utilised in any conceivable actual love relationship. Literary Modernism might be generally characterised as that moment in which the institution of Literature itself became the subject of a squaring operation: $L^2 + L = M$.

Our eye, however, is on post-modernism. Take the suggestion (no more) that 'postmodernism' represents a very late stage in that metaphorical red shift which occurs with each successive iteration of the formula, such that the 'squaring' element in the overall composite result becomes increasingly dominant, outweighing and overwhelming the originating communicative or expressive act. Consider an early example of such a red shift: an oral disputation may be elaborated as a mainly rhetorical exercise (Byzantine public oratory contests) which then perhaps figures as exemplary in pedagogic manuals (Erasmus' *Adages*), becoming thereby the object of student parody and finally of serious satiric appropriation. Another obvious trail would lead from the legal training exercises in the late 16th century Inns of Court and John Donne's apprenticeship as Master of the Revels there to his poetic *Paradoxes*, and perhaps further to Swift's bitter proposals, or Defoe's casuistical case-studies (*Moll Flanders*).

Even the simplest iteration, of course, displaces the utterance from its originating practical context, loosening any relation to specific time and place. As further iterations follow, the red shift tempts us towards conceiving some finally time-less and place-less universality. The impulse towards this red shift may be various, a matter sometimes of what we think of as genre or period. Acrostic or concrete poetry encourages red shift rather more than ballad singing; Baroque taste can tolerate ceilings or epics cluttered with several layers of reworking, allegorised renditions of already mythologised passions, while conversely a classical decorum may spurn all apparent elaboration in favour of a chiselled lucidity and clarity, only a hairsbreadth away from unadorned utterance, stark epitaph or plain prose: here perhaps $a^2 = a$.

Most characteristically, however, within the course of a working lifetime, a practitioner may increasingly prioritise the squaring processes, the repeated reflexive re-iteration of long mastery: a Henry James late novel, the final quartets of Beethoven, the concluding canvases of Turner. Insofar as each component of one's practice is subject to such reflexive elaboration, the result may even look like deconstruction or negation, even incapacity. One motif within postmodernism can then fasten upon such final phases, from whatever period, as exemplary, whether Beckett's rich silences or *The Tempest*'s self-dissolving theatrical bravura and mastery.

Parallel processes in related fields or discourses may also impinge upon and encourage such tendencies, over and above any ageing mastery. Phases in the development of music, philosophy, or criticism might also be mapped according to a similar $[x^2 + x = y]$ formula and the interaction of Thomas Mann, Theodore Adorno and Arnold Schoenberg may then look like a set of simultaneous equations resulting not only in a *Doktor Faustus* but also in a *Moses und Aron* that can no more be a finished opera than the *Aesthetic Theory* can be a systematic theory of aesthetics. The interplay of Eliot, Pound and Joyce as reciprocal critics and mutual models rapidly red-shifted all three through a set of iterations from the already highly reflexive *Waste Land* to the almost end-game of the *Wake* and the self-consciously failed coherence of the *Cantos*.

The relative autonomy of the literary composite, its occupation of an enclosure within its own apparatus, allows the development of a profession (the independent writer) increasingly dependent not upon the personalised reward structures and status of courtier or entertainer, but upon the logics of commodity and publicity. The demands of the culture industry necessitate incessant novelty, the pressure to 'make it new' every season, find new ways of squaring one's own re-iteration. One popular product settles for minimal variation, differently coloured pastimes requiring only minor modifications of the production line (four shades of *Ninja Turtle* or *Power Ranger*, different covers and characters for the same never-ending romance, perhaps several flavours of postmodernism). But beyond the depressing demands of the one-a-season best-seller, the high-status professional operates according to a different (back-list) logic: a pressure towards continual self-refashioning in which the red shift tendency is noticeably accelerated. The pro writer today can enjoy no apocryphal leisured reflection and slow accumulation of masterful technique, with deeply pondered self-improvements enabled by the courtesies of salon criticism; only the late-night cultural chat show asking on publication day what will be different about the *next* novel, the insistent lament of the impatient reviewer that X has merely repeated his previous performance, while each successive blurb promises impossibly new and astonishing innovation. In the competing market of reputation and celebrity, not to have rapidly surpassed one's previous recent best is to fall into forgetfulness. This logic dictates, of course, not whether a work or author is actually read, but only whether the next mountainous pile of mint copies moves sharply off the shelves and into till-receipts.

One important niche market in particular encourages this remorseless self-refashioning: the education-academic sector in which the labour of contemporary canonisation now involves too much cut-throat effort not to be kept firmly profitable by the repeated renewals of any poor writer singled out for the expectant embrace of the curriculum or the conference circuit. Only continual red shift will keep the aspirant to Star Status ahead of the critical competition. Thus, postmodernism doubly beckons. The collusive relation between education and literature stretches back to Homer but the decades since High Modernism have produced an insidious twist which now underpins the postmodernist phase. The academic institutionalisation of professional criticism emerged alongside High Modernism, itself deeply shaped by an almost post-colonial autodidactic pedagogic impulse, painfully apparent in the patricianly educated but culturally insecure American emigré Eliot or the maverick proselytising Euro-modernist Ezra, the uneasily erudite Joyce-Stephen (the first self-conscious undergraduate in fiction), or the class-shaped encounters of a Leonard Bast/Lawrence with the Woolf/Schlegels. The remorseless double trajectory of that symbiosis has made inevitable that aspect of postmodernism which caters to all late-comers to a once apparently impressive cultural feast, until the fruit turns to cinders.

Several phases can be distinguished in the English assimilation of Modernism, modulating into postmodernism. In the first period, from about 1920 to 1945, *Scrutiny* and Leavis established the necessary new bearings, remapping the previous peaks of poetry so that the trail led to Eliot. But by the time this effort was successful, and the university syllabuses and school curricula had duly refocussed round the Metaphysical Poets and *The Waste Land,* the Modernist impulse had already spoken its own elegy in *Four Quartets.* After 1945 a second generation of critics settled into the increasingly professionalised and institutionalised practice of Lit.Crit. Well-trained elucidators got to work, providing ever more minutely explanatory commentaries on every aspect of the Modernist corpus, while leaving contemporary writers in a curious limbo of reputation: too late for Modernism. The third generation, from about 1965 onwards, to whom this elucidatory work had already been so splendidly proferred, therefore faced a dismal dilemma: the Canon and its

Antecedents were now secure and efforts to modify it or prize it open to admit new or allegedly neglected voices, confronted the inertia and self-evident weight of those library shelves by then devoted to Eliot and the Pound Era: no revelation after the death of the last apostle; the pantheon was closed to all but a very few latecomers, Beckett perhaps, but not even Zukovsky.

The aspiring young critic of the 1970s therefore had few avenues to prominence. Merely demolishing reputations would be a *kamikaze* career move. Mildly reinforcing others' canonical work would earn only correspondingly mild respect. To boldly remap the canon, to colonise a new solar system revolving round, say, Hardy or Auden, meant challenging too many senior colleagues still clinging on in the sacred wood. But re-validating their existing valuations in exciting new accents could pay promotional dividends. It was hardly surprising that for a time the young marxist and structuralist warriors re-fought the very same terrain as before, but with more sophisticated weapons. The force of theory was with them, even if for a time the same *Grands Oeuvres* (if not Dead Authors) remained masters of the canonical universe.

Within this overall history the specific function of the postgraduate student of literature has been increasingly important. If metaphysics was once what one studied after taking the physics course, postmodernism was for a time what one encountered after taking the Modernist Finals Paper. Many English departments used to attempt a three-year undergraduate program that covered literature from *Beowulf* to Virginia Woolf but stopped cautiously there, at canon's end. Until the 1970s that pattern left the increasing postgraduate population in need of some fresh challenge that steered a path between merely retracing old syllabus ground and encroaching on the unacceptably contemporary: how with proper self-respect could one possibly either humbly embark on the 400th thesis on George Eliot or giddily risk one's future career prospects on a possibly fleeting figure (would you have written your thesis in 1970 on, say, E. L. Doctorow?). Critical Theory in its various guises provided a respectable enough fresh territory for post-graduate coursework and could also be applied at will throughout the received canon, generating inexhaustible and suitably original reassessments and regroupings. By the 1980s, of course, the proliferation of literatures allied with the new social movements (black, feminist, and gay writing) had eased the demands for untrodden thesis topics and novelty MA programmes, but by then the theoretical habit was engrained. I once sketched a spoof Lacanian reading of *Sir Gawayne and the Green Knight* only to be promptly asked to supervise a thesis on the topic.

Willing postgraduates soon realised that the new Modern Masters of Theory generated reading lists even more formidable than those undergraduate course-work piles of 19th century novel-bricks. With gentle irony I recently asked a postgraduate reading group which met in self-organised weekly sessions why it had taken them a whole ten-week term to get all the way from Descartes to Derrida. Innocent of irony, they admitted "Well, we did spend two weeks on Hegel." Postmodernism, inheriting that precise constituency, often seems to exist primarily as books about Postmodernism targeted at postgraduates and full of such sentences as:

> Philosophically, each orientation has been expressed in ways most relevant to the postmodern debate by Nietzsche (whose radical fictionality can be traced back to Coleridge and forward to Wallace Stevens or Thomas Pynchon or critics such as Ihab Hassan and Frank Kermode's *The Sense of an Ending*) on the one hand, and Heidegger (whose concept of situatedness or Being-in-the-world connects Wordsworth with writers such as Charles Olson or critics such as Susan Sontag) on the other. [*Anon*, p 16]

Discuss! Here summary has become asymptotic skim, but the patent impossibility of adequate competences or actual consensus across such a range relativises all such authoritative authorities. The insouciant scope and blatant eclecticism of postmodernists can then come as a relief from any more specialised apprenticeship demands. As the undergraduate syllabuses of the 1990s were redesigned by that first wave of successful postgraduate postmodernizers the market shifted down a further gear. The proliferation of textbooks, introductions, primers, readers, caters to an educational consumer marooned in the mad expansion of academic cultural publishing, itself part of a wider and more intriguing shift of which postmodernism and its complaints is one symptom.

The problem of periodisation can now be reconsidered, but not in terms of political, economic or philosophical phases and orientations. Rather we can propose as a schematic framework a history of dominant communications systems, or DCSs for convenience. In any period, the current DCS is a complex combinatory of several modes of relationship between (as you will) transmitters and receivers, producers and consumers, forms of distribution and consumption of communication, but within each combinatory one mode or medium of communication is dominant. The obvious major candidates for dominant status would be, in sequence, the oral, the literate, the print, and the audio-visual communications systems. These labels can provisionally operate without elaboration. The basic hypothesis would be that 'literature' has tended to take on a significantly new modality, to emerge revived or reborn, at phases of overlap between dominant communications systems, as one yields place to another, precisely because such shifting and grinding of the tectonic plates of communication provokes and enforces a reflexive reworking of the elements of any practice of social communication, a rapid rise in the red shift, a noticeable acceleration of iterations. Even a Thomas Nashe or Deloney can then rapidly get to d^2.

Thus, Eric Havelock has argued for 'the literate revolution' in 5th century Greece, that moment of overlap between oral continuities and alphabetic record, as generating both Homeric epic as we now have it and the peculiarities of Greek dramatic form. The interface between a manuscript and a print culture is increasingly central to Renaissance studies, from Elizabeth Eisenstein to Arthur Marotti. In both moments, established practices in one DCS migrate into and are transformed by insertion into the newly dominant mode, oral into literate, literate into specifically print modes. Though the interface between overlapping DCSs may not have a decisive effect at the immediate point of technical transition, the newly dominant DCS clearly incorporates within itself the continuing if now increasingly subordinate practices of the previous system: encounters and transpositions, deliberate or involuntary, can thus recur variously throughout a long period of renegotiation, with producers' responses to new modes not necessarily in phase with the continuing expectations or revised reactions of their consumers.

Some simple examples from the manuscript/print overlap: a Wyatt love poem or a Skelton satire may have had determinate targets when circulated in manuscript in Henry VIII's court, but their printed publication transformed them both into oddly veiled enigmas. An instructive case would be that of Thomas Whythorne, constrained to explain away (not least to his wife) the provenance of his love poems once they were incorporated into an autobiography intended for printed distribution. Shakespeare's *Sonnets* can arguably be read not as a deeply problematic self-investigation but as a canny commercial exploitation of the print medium to provide a comprehensive collection of hand-me-down verses suitable for any occasion. Somewhat later, Fielding can still successfully mock, in *Shamela*, the impossible conflation of speaking, writing, and print modes in the 'writing to the minute' practices of that master printer, Samuel Richardson, who had reinvented the novel by similarly trying to provide a collection of off-the-shelf correspondence models or templates. Dominance varies, of course: even forty years ago my Latin teacher still thought of Virgil's *Aeneid* as primarily suitable for memorised recitation (he could recite the whole poem backwards) whereas today my own students can find it almost beyond belief that Donne's sonnets should be declaimed aloud, let alone sung.

On the largest scale, there have, it seems, been just three epochal transformations or decisive general shifts between Dominant Communication Systems: those between oral and literate, literate and print, print and audio-visual. That last overlap was characterised by the emergence of photography, sound recording, telephones, radio, cinema, television and video in a protracted renegotation with print forms, from newspapers to novels. Arguably one crucial constituent of High Modernism was its deeply ambivalent response to the impact of audio-visual reproduction upon that print-based prestige culture which so attracted the autodidact in a Pound or Joyce. Eliot could still propose an arduous apprenticeship in the British Museum Reading Room and be scornful of mere typists who put records on gramophones, but meanwhile Joyce was also managing the first cinema in Dublin and Pound exploring the dangerous powers of radio. Later critics would for a time resent and resist film and television as the main cultural enemy, until semiotic theoreticians could cleverly reincorporate the audio-visual according to linguistic premises.

But here a further ambivalence emerges, haunting late modernist modes. Since the 1960s have we witnessed another modulation of either the print system or the audio-visual mode, or are we in a more radical phase of transition to a quite new dominance, a new DCS entirely? This piece is being composed not on a typewriter but in a word-processing program on a multimedia computer. As I write, the computer can play a CD and display a live television picture in a screen window. Has the computer displaced print, television, or both? During its first decades the computer seemed merely a fast replacement for the abacus or graph-paper, a mathematical tool. But increasingly in the 1970s scaled down yet more powerful computers colonised the realm of the typewriter (word-processing) and the printing house (desktop publishing). By the 1980s the command-line interface, keyboard and programming languages were ceding ground to graphical user interfaces, the mouse and object-oriented programming. It is even plausible to map the computer wars between IBM and Macintosh user-preferences as already a contest between Modernist and Postmodernist mind-sets, as Sherry Turkle has proposed. But by the 1990s the personal computer had effectively been re-shaped as an audio-visual machine, a configuration of digital sound and video on the verge of displacing not only the typewriter but also the television set and, coupled with a modem, the telephone also. Most recently the Internet has moved increasingly into audio-visual rather than text-based mode, while CD-ROMs have begun to challenge the book, whether as encyclopaedia or art history, adventure novel or children's story. As usual in an overlap period, the interaction is not just in technology (the global battle for chips and screen standards) but deeply in style and appearance: the look and feel of children's television, of adverts, even documentaries, imitates the design of multi-media screens.

If, however, we have so far tried, according to our hypothesis, to situate significant literary innovation at the point of interface between oral/literate, manuscript/print and print/audio-visual, several questions now arise concerning our current 'dominant communication system'. How far is a communications combinatory dominated by the computer a radically new DCS or just the extension of an older system? How far do current developments prompt us to reconsider the very notion of successive communications systems? Or the slippery notion of dominance? And within this, what is the impact upon what we think of as 'literature'?

A less linear version of the DCS hypothesis would clearly be possible, with its own consequences for locating both 'literature' and 'postmodernism'. Arguably, the continuing groundbase of all communication has always been a combinatory of the oral and the audio-visual, those forms of communication most directly involving the bodily apparatus itself. The popular, widespread, easily accessible modes of communication have always revolved round speech and spectacle, from face to face conversation or campfire recitation, through the proliferation of oral performances and visual displays that sustained the ideological hold of the mediaeval church, in preaching and stained glass, passion plays and liturgical processions, to that vivid combination of speech and vision which is television. By contrast, what has marked both written and printed forms, the one as mere variant of the other, is an exclusiveness and association with restricted access, an alliance with elitist patterns of power and control. Complications multiply in any detailed account and such a broad generality may be worth too little, but rather than a four-stage succession, this emphasis would propose a long wave of audio-visual development, with a perhaps only short-term phase of writing/printing superimposed upon it for a while.

Those few centuries which link Renaissance, Enlightenment and Modernism were centrally constituted by a print-oriented problematic, focussed variously upon the possible democratisations of, or dangers to, intellect and knowledge from widely distributed and uniform written language, text-objects. Within the written/print mode several entwined issues arose: the emphasis on epistemological certainty, and the need for explicitly declared starting points for argument or inquiry, emerges as a feature of written and particularly printed discourse. Spoken exchange does not require or even tolerate a definitive starting point and is impatient with issues of epistemological validation (any such argument being resolved by dismissive persuasion, sharp verbal practice, abrupt discontinuation, or at worst resort to on-the-spot anger).

A book, between fixed covers and with determinate pages glued into order, circulating in a public sphere of impersonal scrutiny, unmoored from any immediate context of dialogical disputation, needs to establish and justify its opening gambits, its premises and conclusions, to contain and exhaustively account for its sources and evidence. A book's procedures and the scope of its expertise must be explicit, listed, itemised, tabulated, indexed, available for suspicious examination, guarded pre-emptively against all potential assault. Our print-oriented notions of 'literature' (the term is eloquent) derive from that phase of self-sustaining book practice, the closed artefact, autotelic, organic, stable, shaped to effective closure. 'Literature' has difficulties with open form and improvised modes, from theatrical performance to folk tale, from public pageant to the daily flow of television. Post-print philosophy, like Mallarmé's poetry, aspires to put the world in a book, but a pub argument can develop as it will, turning responsively to unexpected opponents or supporters, a *bricolage* of temporary holding points, a repertoire of fast-footed moves, its confrontational eyes on the disputed end-topic not on any expediently shared temporary consensus along the way. Similarly a great oral story teller, whether of feudal epic or urban anecdote, can adjust constantly to the living crowd rather than respect formal niceties and consistencies.

Postmodernism may soberly cite its scholarly origins in a crisis of bibliographical expansion, but its true affinities are surely with the old ploys of the oral performer, the playful patter of jester-courtier, conjuror or quack doctor, the immediately plausible polemics of practising barrister, politician or preacher. Transposed onto the page, of course, these loosely flexible modes may also look like post-Modernist literary elaborations, but such shape-shifting and elusive forms decline to be encapsulated in any genre definition. If Adorno could characterise the modernist composition as one which generated the uniquely specific rules by which it demanded to be judged, the postmodernist artefact endeavours a rule-less self-configuration. To capture postmodernism itself in any general net of specifying features, even this one, would then break that very rule. But what now confronts postmodernism is a double dilemma. With Modernism, one might suggest, the process of literary squaring had already reached, perhaps, M, half-way through the notional alphabet soup of my formula. Postmodernism was tempted to attempt that further step, the impossible Q^2 of total self-reflexive *aporia*. But for that the launch-pad of print's own highpoints were still required, yet that very inheritance of print culture, of higher education, was endangered by a new-old competitor.

At first computers could be securely assimilated to that restrictive tradition of specialist skills and arcane knowledges, in continuity with established guilds of scribes and clerics. Mastery of a programming language or fluency with a command line interface required a learning curve akin to that of learning to read or write, but while schools increasingly despaired of teaching even basic book-skills juvenile hackers and joyous games-masters exposed as doubly hollow the specious political promises that conscientious computer literacy would ensure profitable employment. The rapid de-skilling of all computer-assisted competences, so that almost everyone could now almost paint, compose music, engineer an environment or plan a city, coupled with the internet dissemination of newly public information channels beyond the control and constraint of formal educational structures, has left the privileged inheritors of print peculiarly precarious, despite valiant attempts to adapt traditional literary forms as computer based inter-active fiction or to seek new alliances between Critical Theory and hyper-text. The literary postgrad may now be a terminally doomed species, except as continuing cover and cloak for youth unemployment. The next iteration of communication processes may not involve further refinements of any writing devices of Modernism but a fresh start in the new fields of MM: multi-media. In designing a CD-ROM or on-line encyclopaedia for children today it is neither knowledge experts nor practised writers whose work is at a premium, but the combinatory talents of computer graphic artists, digital video editors and MacroMedia directors. And, as with previous major transitions, a new 'aesthetic' is urgently on the agenda: nobody now has a clue what a major multimedia masterpiece would look/sound like. We are back to square one.

Yet the signs of the times remain uncertain. Is the computer, as the frontier scouts of cyberspace proclaim, carrying us all (some earlier than others) into a new era, of liberated information, electronic gift-exchange, artifically intelligent agencies, pollution-free nanotechnology, artificial life forms, and global community? Is this a new epochal Renaissance, or just the technology and social relations of the industrial-capitalist period reaching its always-inevitable apogee of unparalleled global disparities—or is it all merely the passing fag-end of a brief century deceived yet again by its own utopian hype and hypocrisies? To return to our opening question, it is not after all surprising that attempts to define, describe, encapsulate these dwindling decades of the twentieth century in a pithy phrase should have produced so persistently ambiguous a term as 'postmodernism'.

Meanwhile, the culture industry has its own momentum: the matrix stirs, the kaleidoscope of consumerism shakes. After four or more flavours of postmodernism, the market is a little tired. And in any case since 1989 the politics have also shifted: the world (or the bit of it that thinks of itself as the world) no longer needs to deny the possibility of Grand Narratives: it can now write its own again, safe from marxism. Like all fading product lines, postmodernism may now try to postpone the end-of-season sale, holding back the historically inevitable, even denying history itself. But yesterday it was post this and that; tomorrow the internet, or virtual reality, or nano-technology. Bill Gates is buying the digital rights to the million best pictures, worth more than any words. Now we know what comes 'after Literature'.

*

CYBERTHEORY

Old Trains Of Thought

I have for a long time written satirical and political ballads and indeed performed them. Perhaps when I first began to write 'serious criticism', I never really saw a way of hooking that up with such more popular kinds of cultural activity. I would hope that, now, there is in my writing an attempt at a greater convergence between the two. And the same really applies to my novel: I was delighted when somebody said that what they liked about it was that, although it was an intellectual novel, it was not an academic novel. . . So, once again, to try to write, as they say, creatively but also intellectually would be a desirable stylistic and political goal. I am horrified by the dearth of ideas in contemporary English fiction, which I think has its roots in a certain ingrown English empiricism and commonsensicality, and I think that if there is to be a viable fiction of the left, as well as a theory, then it has to find ways of bringing creative and intellectual discourses together.

I was reading that final paragraph of Terry Eagleton's recent book. *The Significance of Theory*, while sitting in a train stalled at Nuneaton station. After I closed the book came the ritual of pondering.

That provincial Midland town of Nuneaton, outside my window, was where the young Marian Evans grew up, on her way to becoming the exemplarily mature George Eliot, author of *Middlemarch*, the quintessential novel of Leavis's great tradition, linchpin of EngLit courses for a generation. But she was also author of that major attempt at English intellectual political fiction, *Daniel Deronda*, selectively excised by the same F. R. Leavis, to be reconstituted and tamed as *Gwendolen Harleth*. As the train waited, I measured in memory the density of those great Victorian novels, their pace and length, the sense of journey embedded in their very structure, their linear narration and closure, their obvious relation to this very railway system which emerged with them and helped sustain them. Once, long ago, back in the early 1960s, in *The Long Revolution*, Raymond Williams had analysed the 1840s sales figures for novels sold on W.H. Smith's new railway kiosks as a way into explaining the 'structure of feeling' of a historical moment. I remembered the difficulty, and therefore the excitement, then, of advancing such analyses, entwining material history and critical analysis into a single argument, itself a step on the way to recognising the formal structuring of such fiction by its own modes of production, distribution and consumption. Familiar and now faded modes of theory. The cover of Terry Eagleton's very first book, endearingly entitled *The New Left Church*, included a picture of a railway station. Inside was a laconic analysis of how modern railways symbolised both connection and alienation, as a prelude to close 'practical criticism' of the structure of feeling in then-contemporary poetry. Very New Left. Very early Marx.

Marian Evans, *en route* to becoming George Eliot, moved from provincial backwater to national reputation via responsibility for a metropolitan journal, as effective editor of the *Westminster Review*. The journal as means of intervention and as defining a generation now has a long tradition. I still have a complete set of *Scrutiny* and a very long run of *New Left Review* (*NLR*). In 1968 *NLR*'s editor Perry Anderson 'placed' F.R. Leavis as neatly as he might have done it himself: a map of British culture centred on a displaced totalisation, literary criticism, itself to be displaced by the deliberate pantheon of New Left Books' continental translations throughout the 1970s. But Anderson's account left out both creative literature and the hard sciences: it was our 'concepts of man and society' that were crucial, and lacking. A severe dose of high theory was peremptorily prescribed. The piece was reprinted recently, in Anderson's *English Questions*, but even in its sequel, 'A culture in counterflow', Anderson's map still omits theatre, film and television as well as science. It also relegates to a single footnote the true theoretical successor to *NLR* itself, the *Screen* of the 1970s.

In my own university 'English' has remained largely uninfluenced by any explicit literary theory, but in the 1970s Kent set up degrees in Marxist studies and in women's studies, a drama degree heavily influenced by Williams, and a film studies course staffed by *Screen* editors. Then in the 1980s came a Lacan-inspired MA in psychoanalytic studies, a Board of Post-Colonial Studies and a BA in a home-grown hybrid, 'Communications & Image Studies'. Before getting on the train today I went to the railway bookstall, to buy not a novel or *NLR* but *Amiga Format* and *Byte*. Some years ago I stopped teaching literature and literary theory. Now I chair that multidisciplinary degree programme, 'communications and image studies', and spend much of my time initiating students into the multimedia possibilities of computers interfacing with video and sound. The long crawl of the inter-city train gave me a chance to read the latest computer news and, for a while, *The Significance of Theory*.

(Several years ago an EngLit colleague turned up for a meeting white-faced. On inquiry his shock turned out to be caused not by news of cancer or redundancy but by an idle moment of calculation: he had just given his five hundredth supervision on Middlemarch.)

Memories of Theories And Practices

So what now is the significance of theory? Part of the difficulty is knowing what theory is being contrasted with. The older formulations of a polarity of theory and practice tended to be dependent upon the theoretical position one adopted. If theory meant Marxism, the appropriate practice was to do with political revolution, with a definable agency, victim and purpose. If one's theoretical allegiance was primarily to psycho-analysis, the paradigmatic practice was ultimately the clinical. The chain of links between theory and practice might then stretch somewhat unconvincingly across several layers of other theory/practice couplings, negotiated step by step. At present, however, it seems that theory does not so readily, or guiltily, distinguish itself from practice, but rather assimilates practice into itself: the practice of writing being itself responsible, it can seem, for the construction of agencies and audiences, a self-generating auto-gestion. If, for Anderson, literary criticism was a substitute totalisation, at least the kind of totalisation involved was in continuity with George Eliot's own: the ambition to make sense of a whole society, historically, sociologically and culturally. Marx could share that arena with Eliot's novels and Marxists could self-persuasively align their functions as intellectuals with the places already prepared for the English 'cultural critic'. Williams had traced that lineage in his *Culture and Society* and located himself within it. But an old impasse had always been there.

(At the launch meeting of the May Day Manifesto, in 1968, Williams, as editor, outlined its process of collaborative composition, recalling the long weekend of final paste-up: how the various single-issue analyses and expert local contributions, as they were placed next to each other on his table at home, had finally converged and intertwined, leading unmistakably towards political conclusion and stance, which in turn led, as the argument unfolded and spread along the table, to the inevitable question of agency and strategy . . . 'There,' Williams concluded enigmatically, 'the table ended.')

The once-dominant model (call it Model T) of the relation between theory and practice saw theory as a prerequisite and preliminary to practice; theory produced and informed analysis, and without analysis no appropriate practice was possible. This model had its roots in the Marxist distinction between the underlying causal forces within a social formation (mapped as the economy) and the more dependent cultural components of that formation (base and superstructure). It was then the task of theoreticians (an aspect of all political activists) to understand those underlying forces, and this allegedly qualified them for correct strategic insight, equipping them with a surer basis for tactical intervention and influence.

From *The Long Revolution* (*LR*) onwards one can trace in Williams's work the demolition of the foundations of this whole model. Yet at the same time the very format of his work re-enacted much the same basic model. In *LR* a theoretical first section was followed by several chapters of history, themselves succeeded by proposals and policies for the present. The implication of this formal arrangement was linear and hierarchical: establish the theory first, see the historical connections, and then move to current practice. The very ambition of the historical chapters indicated one of the persistent problems of this model even within a formal pedagogy: an unavoidably asymptotic curve on the historical material needing to be mastered. Any attempt to build, say, an interpretation of Jacobean drama on the foundations established by historical research rapidly embroiled one in the battles between sharply differing historians; either one's delayed and provisional contribution became merely that of an amateur onlooker waiting to see who had won, or one offered the analysis of the 'literature' also as one more contribution to the historical debate, a conflation of genres and disciplines that could end only with assimilation. A similar problem persisted for any theoretically informed politics: the endlessly procrastinated and asymptotic process of analytical 'rigour' that would finally pinpoint the revolutionary moment.

(I once asked a student who had already done a highly specialised MA in Victorian literature, and was now taking a 'special period' paper 1830-70, whether he would prefer to concentrate on one or two authors, say Tennyson or Clough. 'Does Tennyson come into that period?' he asked.)

At a broad level, what succeeded this basic model did indeed collapse genre and discipline distinctions, as it did the relation between theory and practice. The initially influential version of this model (call it Model S) was Althusserian in tenor, and its most severe British manifestation signalled the appropriate shift in the very title of its inevitable journal: *Theoretical Practice*. Central to this still influential family of approaches and positions (theories) has been the notion that a social or discursive formation is at some level intra-dependently systemic, and that the linchpins of any such system are at root conceptual. In so far as the entire social order is theoretically characterised by one or two key organising principles, by a specific epistemic configuration, or by the spectacle or the simulacrum, any opponent is also recognised as a participant: the situationist is also a spectacle, Baudrillard is undeniably a simulacrum. This stance has one of its roots in Surrealism: the construction of a self-sustaining artefact enjoying a displaced and displacing relation to what one might otherwise have simple-mindedly thought of as the real: the surreal offers not so much an alternative world as a disorienting recognition of the genuine oddity of the apparent world. The crucial practice is then a kind of theory, conceptual intervention, yet problematic, even pessimistic, since the very notion of agency tends to dissolve, while the issue of historical change and succession is rendered almost unthinkable. A long sequence of theoretical fashions, from Lévi-Strauss to Lacan, from Foucault to a resuscitated Debord, from Orientalism to Exterminism, can be grouped under this general rubric (Saussurean/structuralist/semiotic/ situationist, etc.).

Some of Terry Eagleton's later books bear a somewhat similar relation to this second strand of theoretical model as Williams's *Long Revolution* did to the first: a kind of textual counter-positioning. For example. *The Function of Criticism* is organised as a historical working through of the logic of 'criticism', from its inauguration in the public sphere of eighteenth-century journals and coffee houses to the present professionalised ghetto of conference papers and university departments. Yet in so far as the book's argument demonstrates that there is no longer a public sphere within which and through which criticism can have a political function and effect, the book thereby underwrites its own lack of function and becomes an artefact curiously held up only by its own creation of an audience, a kind of autotelic state of reproduction. Subsequently, and appropriately, *The Ideology of the Aesthetic* replays at a more overtly philosophical level the trajectory sketched more locally in Williams's *Culture and Society*, but both seem over-indebted to a historical moment of mediation that has now passed. Both Marxist and Conservative uses of aesthetics and culture derive, arguably, not so much from Romanticism or German Idealist theory but from a phase in mid-Victorian England when the crucial and pragmatic ideological function of 'culture' was to help compose a single hegemonic block, by reconstituting a common class identity for the successors of the two contending classes of the long revolution of the eighteenth century. (By this time my train was passing through Rugby: faint echoes of Tom Brown's miserable public school days, of Thomas Arnold and his sad sons.) But as organised democratic demands successfully extended the formal franchise, that reliance on culture as hegemonising cement was transmuted. From being an inward constitutive of a new ruling class self-consciousness and sensibility, 'culture' was increasingly offered, in the mass newspapers of the nineteenth century and the mass media of the twentieth, as an external and so-called 'national heritage', dangled discriminatingly before an 'uncultured' subordinate class but with the promise of incorporation and assimilation.

The underlying move here was effectively to separate knowledge from power, to offer an unprecedented dramatising of society freely available to all citizens, manufacturing an imagined community across a national breakfast table or television tray, yet at the same time to restrict any actual engagement in political decision-making to an occasional intervention in the private election booth. Within this process, the deeply identificatory effect of those literary devices of totalisation, linearity, and closure became sufficiently generalised and incorporated into the popular generic forms of the new media as to make actual literature largely redundant, and as 'Literature' became marginalised, so did the critical function of debate around literature.

Any radical dissenter still operating from within that inherited arena had to retrain as an expert combatant in general semiotic systems. Whereas Williams could, initially, speak from within a secure territorial base and a known community allegiance (not least as a historical novelist of an ambitiously totalising kind), Eagleton had the generationally later task of becoming an assault commando in a cultural no man's land, a cyberspace cowboy of the intellectual matrix, attacking the shifting theoretical ice of artificially intelligent ideological formations, assaulting the institutionally entrenched defence systems of capitalist academia, hacking into the secret spaces and inner recesses of ideological manufacture, exposing its trade secrets and advance sales strategies. It was invigorating but sometimes seemed like misplaced energy: dammit, why didn't he write about politics instead?

(I once asked Terry why he wanted to write a book on Walter Benjamin. So that the New York Review of Books doesn't get there first, was the reply.)

Postbinaries: From *The Sun* to Sony and Sun Systems

As literary criticism glided from theory to theory to meta-theory, one response argued that the appropriate targets in this sophisticated war of position were not the Metaphysical poets and John Bayley, or even the metaphysics of presence, but nationalist myopia and Rupert Murdoch and, for example, the *Sun*'s advertising pages as the self-representation of capitalist commodification. Nevertheless, even a semiotic deconstruction of a Chanel advert or a page three girl was hardly likely to undermine the grip of Saatchi and Saatchi, let alone NATO, and, as a recent massive volume testifies, that moment has produced its own uninspiring professional impasse: an academicisation of 'popular culture' that leaves one still in a spectatorial stance, facing yet again the issues of enablement and empowerment, of strategy and perspective.

What now tends to be offered as alternatives to this old impasse are feminist criticism, with its alternatives to the received canon of both texts and paradigm practices, and some notion of 'postmodernist' criticism or theory. Both these proffered alternatives may, however, be only yet further variations on the basic pattern of the two earlier models: feminism as allocating a new group allegiance, yet locating oppression still in some underlying distribution of powers which needs prior reform before the more super-structural features of the oppressive universe are alterable; the postmodernists offering only updated formulae of totality, of ostensibly self-sustaining discursive formations which yet have to be somehow overturned or sabotaged by the very sustainers themselves.

If we want to think outside these parameters, if there is an emergent third model of 'theory' with some relation to what used to be literary theory, it may be useful to recall that earlier models of literary theory were connected to changes in two other fields: in literary production and in pedagogic practices. There was indeed a line that stretched from railways through three-decker novels to Leavis, just as there was also an overlap between the new poetry of modernism, the emphasis on individual teaching supervisions, and the practice of close reading. If we now consider the significant literature of the past decade or so, it is arguable that one symptomatic genre has been cyberpunk fiction, as a focus for and articulation of several other developments, in hard science and in popular culture. Noticeably, it is one mode of writing that conflates both the areas omitted from Anderson's original map: fiction and hard science. It also directly connects to changes in the overall pedagogic situation, to the emergence of quite new technologies of social communication, information storage and intellectual production, themselves part of the social and industrial shifts which undermined both older class allegiances and the binary global oppositions of the Cold War epoch. The trains of the nineteenth-century industrial revolution are finally being replaced by the faxlines and satellite computer communication networks of the late twentieth century. Neither Marx nor Saussure can easily cope. By now this information revolution is no longer a matter for speculation or spectatorship even by literary academics, but deeply constitutive of the position we occupy precisely as academics and also as citizens. For what is at stake in these new developments is another epochal change in relations between knowledge and power, including those defining the status of the academy within a wider society.

We can single out three elements characteristic of the cyberpunk genre and its associated scientific developments. One is the dissolution of previous distinctions and divisions in computer design itself between hardware and software, with the 'connectionist' model of computer seeking to incorporate self-modifying neural networks, to enable a learning process to occur through use rather than (as with any *langue: parole* model) the hardwiring of generalised rules upon which to operate specific application routines. The basic model here is the human brain itself. Second is the notion of the matrix, the shared information space accessible to any participant. By jacking into the computer networks, thereby joining the brain's own neural net into that of the matrix, the cyber-rider effaces that other distinction between human and machine, and potentially therefore that between intellectual and manual labour which, for example, underpins the binary distinctions still deployed in that opening passage from Eagleton. Third, within the matrix, as with any hyper-organised system, the end of linearity is inevitable. Connections are no longer necessarily hierarchically structured but mappable as potential cross-linkings which conform to no previously prescribed or authorised pathways. The matrix explorer thus becomes an interactive agent rather than a follower of routes established by precedents or instructors. The moral panic aroused by hacking has its unavoidable basis here.

These features of the new information pattern have direct implications for pedagogy, some of which are already operative at primary and secondary levels, if not in most university English departments. What is involved is a real change in relations of authority and knowledge within pedagogy. If students now have desktop access to far more information than any teacher can hope to know, or check, if the entire Library of Congress can now, or shortly, sit on a few CD-ROMS in a work cubicle, how can accredited knowledge status and formal expertise be exercised as control? And if the received hierarchies of organisation of knowledge are open to multiple modification through personalised search and retrieval routines, how can any canon or discipline of relevance be effectively maintained? Already in primary and secondary schools the advent of the personal computer has redefined the classroom task more as one of guidance in the use of resources for searching out knowledge than as transmitting intellectual content.

(A friend teaching in a small rural school in the United States writes that the school has just bought, for toddler use, more Apple Macintosh computers than my university's computing lab has.)

One could, of course, link these developments back to older issues. The proliferation of computer networks, bulletin boards and electronic mail facilities might raise again the possibility of forms of public sphere, of non-territorial equal-access communication communities in quite new forms. The development of virtual reality technologies echoes some of the concerns of the Surrealists. The overlap between advanced computer research and immediate applications in the leisure and entertainment fields poses questions about the relation between popular and elite cultures: is learning the Amiga games-programming program *Amos* an elite educational activity or a street hobby? Brecht's account in *Galileo* of the dockyard mechanic instructing the philosopher in new methods of calculation might be recalled here.

To some extent these developments may also recast our sense of previous forms of communication, storage and expression: we might now see the organising structure of Herbert's *The Temple* as that of a hypertext, or recognise the intense reading of a novel as an early form of jacking into a shared cyberspace or virtual reality, while some scholars have seen medieval uses of memory as akin to our own deployment of AI machines. The *HyperCard* program given away with every Macintosh computer can familiarise users with concepts of inter-textuality and polyphonic reading that might once have figured in a seminar on Derrida. It was pleasantly predictable that Coleridge should figure as patron of some of these developments: Ted Nelson has named his proposed universal hyper-book 'Xanadu'. For just as one might see some older literature in these new terms, so these new developments can be seen as indebted to long-familiar modes of literary composition and comprehension: much modernist writing has already explored post-linear, polyphonic modes of organisation and of understanding: *The Waste Land*, as Ike Achebe has neatly shown, was always a kind of multimedia hypertext. The spatial form of the nineteenth-century novel itself could even be seen as anticipating the virtual acres of multiply-interconnecting databases. The notion of the matrix can be related to T. S. Eliot's insistence on having the whole of European art in one's very bones, while his notion of individual talent as effecting a shift in the internal relations of every pre-existing text can now be realised in the dynamic update features of multi-tasking operating systems.

(One student of mine has found it easy and logical to move from research on reading strategies in Finnegans Wake to designing human-computer interfaces in a research lab.)

In this brave new cyber-world some of the once merely ancillary skills taught on EngLit degree courses may now move more centre stage. The discipline of bibliographical citation extends into online data-base searching; with scanners and optical character recognition the problems of sloppy note-taking and of plagiarism are transmuted into concerns that echo Walter Benjamin's dream of a text composed entirely of quotations; the writing of coursework essays becomes the composing of multimedia scripts. Educational production increasingly joins hands with those enjoyable forms of prosumer home production: video-editing and electronic music composition, bedroom studio-recording and public domain or open source software-programming. Once students are encouraged by the very storage mechanisms available to them to create their own idiosyncratic interconnections, rather than follow structured reading lists and syllabuses, the contribution of the teacher fades and with it those related hierarchies of theory and practice, the prioritising of preliminary theoretical clarification and allegiance. What replaces them may be only the simple but difficult awareness of the dense multitude of possible uses and reformulations of any text, including one's own word-processed rewrite of it.

There is of course an immediate and unwelcome political context within which some of these changes are currently being introduced into the educational system, by a government anxious to cheapen education in every sense, to cram undergraduate degrees into two years, to increase staff:student ratios and to reduce research facilities. More widely, only a small percentage even of the developed world has these technologies available, and endorsement of these directions can seem a matter solely of parochial privilege. Yet it is only ten years since the BBC introduced the first schools computer and a mere six or so since the user-friendly Mac interface appeared. The pace of innovation and penetration has been remarkable. The whole of Greek and Latin literature, including translations and lexicons, together with, for example, detailed maps and visual information on archaeological sites, can now be accessed on interactive laser disc. Much of English literature can now be downloaded in machine readable form. Secondary school pupils can now edit and publish via e-mail a European-wide school newspaper. Precisely because new pedagogic practices always underpin new theories, it is premature to extrapolate to the new theories likely to emerge in the near future, but involved in these technical possibilities is potentially a real transformation, beyond the myopically limited priorities and perspectives of a cost-cutting government. Historically, revolutions involve a deep change in perceptions of the world and in taken-for-granted premises, and these recent technical possibilities do imply a set of shifts on a par with those associated with the invention of print, perhaps even a change in human self-perception as far-reaching as the decentring of helio-centric man, as our notion of intelligence shifts to accommodate artificial intelligence. The materialism of the 1970s put the material body, of sexuality and biology, on to the political agenda, but the material structure of the brain itself is now crucial to the new developments.

Williams actually began *The Long Revolution* with an attempt to understand the notion of creativity in terms of J.Z. Young's work on the brain. He would presumably now begin from the more recent work on neural nets. If there is an underlying 'theory', that is perhaps where to locate it. But, in increasingly actual practice, the perspective available to us now is of an even longer revolution than Williams's, one in which at a point beyond current criteria of material sufficiency we can move towards a form of accessible electronic wealth, of values and pleasures located in information access and production. Even within the brief history and current limitations of the hardware, tens of millions already have personal computers that do not simply keep accounts or word-process but can play games, make music, paint, capture images and sounds. What was once the preserve of a few specialists in the various fields is now available even on the shelves of W.H. Smith. The latest issue of *Amiga Shopper* includes a program for constructing your own neural network. Within a few years the everyday games machine may be as powerful as today's SUN workstation, the domestic video recorder as sophisticated as the professional Sony systems in broadcast use now. When writing interactive online fiction is as common a practice as taking family snaps, or composing multi-track music is no more mysterious than dialling a telephone number, then 'literature' will perhaps have finally lost its last aura and become a genuinely secular, and democratic, activity. In the medieval monastery to read a text was to transcribe it, meditatively, for a month or more. That practice survived the printing press no more successfully than reading five-hundred-page novels on the train will outlast the laptop.

(George Eliot, so the story goes, had tears running down her cheeks as she persisted with the translation of Strauss's Life of Jesus, knowing that the object of her faith was dissolving under her pen. She would look up from her desk to the crucifix upon her wall and pray to the Christ whose life was being demythologised by her own work. As I write this on my home computer I can see the books I write on it fading into antiquity even as I write them.)

Travelling Theory

The train is moving again. Looking out of the window I am aware of the continuing deep influence of a certain reading of Marx. What I see is not only a natural beauty but worked land deeply formed by generations of labour, the material world as human product. As the train travels through that laboured land I recall Williams's texts on city and country, on known and unknown communities, his plays about the railways his father worked on in Pandy, with Tintern Abbey a few miles away. But now, with a changed attention, I find myself looking much more within the carriage, at the other people around me, and particularly at the children, aware of them too as the products of a certain kind of sustained and difficult labour, each child as formed not only from parental labour but as the end product of an immensely long yet also incredibly specific history, older than the most ancient heritage: the unique combination of a particular double lineage of DNA, of an unrepeatable configuration of neural nets and of a densely detailed personal history knowable only, if at all, in the strange territories of individual psychoanalysis.

What is then profoundly ironic in the present context of government education policy, ostensibly preoccupied with economising and productivity, with waste of public resources and inefficient use of plant, is the immense waste of these incredibly sophisticated biocomputers, equipped with a nanotechnology older than empires and more powerful than a super Cray computer. These individual people, including me and my children, are the most extraordinary resource any community could want, yet the social formation that shapes us also wastes our immense potential of uniqueness.

Old habits die hard. I idly elaborate an insight into ideology: that all infants really have to believe that the world makes sense, since they are actually making sense of it as they grow—the development of their brain's neural network allows them no alternative; thus, given the kinds of actual environment children may have to make sense of, any system at all, however bizarre, can become the truth for them, even the paranoid culture and profligate economy of commodity capitalism. Perhaps, after all, education and family upbringing, those traditional emphases of the Right, are indeed more crucial than such relatively variable factors as the role of the working class or the function of intellectuals. Class, after all, is not only where you come from but where your kids are going. Yet the present social structure is so patently unstable and unpredictable, the present pace of scientific and technological development so rapid and unforeseeable, that it is even more impossible now to forecast where one's kids might one day find themselves. Railways opened up a new expanse of geographical mobility; my own working-class generation saw a new range of social mobility; now, my children will have available to them as a future form of mobility a kind of cyberspace travel that I can barely conceive.

The urgent agenda in my view, therefore, concerns not the elaboration of yet another theory of literary production or practice, but the provision of an entire education appropriate to a generation who will outlive our very notions of intelligence, information, education. Older theories tended to be correlated with certain models of both pedagogy and writing. The first, basically economistic, model of theory often had its practical counterpart in the claim that what is wrong with education is a lack of resources. If only we could get the economy right, or enough teachers, or enough computers, then the students would follow, either in appropriate numbers (the government's concern) or desirable quality. A parallel with certain writing practices might be suggested, where the concern was to invest in a lifetime labour of scholarship and research before venturing to offer a cautious critical interpretation, or, at under-graduate level, to do the 'period' properly before you could understand the poem. I once wrote a hundred pages on one brief poem by Yeats; forty of them were about the economic history of Ireland.

The second model of theory went with, or goes with, a situation in which teaching centres primarily on a text (literary or itself theoretical), now offered without reference to any specific historical context and often taught by a teacher who has no specific responsibility for the institutional context of that teaching. A fairly widespread model now in the States is that of the visiting guru parachuting in to give a prestige seminar or lecture series; this often produces what I think of as helicopter theory. The writing practice correlative to this theoretical stance tends to offer self-sustaining verbal icons as the preferred product model. I once wrote a five hundred page book which essentially held itself up by a number of internal dialectical structures. I then wrote a small book that included a variety of texts which had no reality other than that given by their imagined reviews in a fictive journal. Both books formally incorporated a dominant institutional device, the education apparatuses and the critical review, and though I hope readers derived some pleasure and amusement, I doubt if either book was ever of much direct use to anyone.

The third model, or lack of one, that I want to propose is more like the *bricolage* of the home-video enthusiast who has to put together the bedroom computerised editing suite with whatever connections, leads, adapters and cables are to hand; the pedagogical equivalent is allowing students to become adept at constructing their own multi-disciplinary curriculum, designed not for now but for about twenty years into an unknowable future. The writing component of such work is not the publishing of books but the drafting of degree programmes and course outlines. The proliferation of new degree courses and programmes, at Kent and elsewhere, seems increasingly the right area into which to put one's energies.

How, then, should I write this contribution to the 'state of theory', the title of this symposium? As an elaborated theoretical justification of that stance? As simply a list of resources? As an outline of a particular degree structure? Or perhaps, in deference to an older mode, as a meditative reflection, itself a kind of neural net, taking shape on a journey, a structure for discoveries rather than a predigest of conclusions, not so much a history or narrative as a frame for a few anecdotes, themselves nodes for new connections, switches and signals, repetitions and variations, weighted interlinkages, semantic nets, hidden layers? The neural net offers no single command economy, no organising consciousness over and above the net itself. The hardest task of all, pedagogically, theoretically, politically, may be to abandon the old radical desire for totalisation while not falling back into a parochially pragmatic concern or a tamed and muted area of special interest ('literary theory 1968-90');

rather, to design an open structure which recognises that precisely because 'Literature' was always, potentially, about everything, a 'literary' education now might involve work not just on narrative but on nuclear power, not only on women writers but on neural nets, not just on spatial form but on hyperspace. The equivalent of 'literary theory' might then be simply a set of enabling navigation tools, a backpack for cultural production.

One of the great strengths of Raymond Williams, in face-to-face teaching, was his refusal of the familiar temptation to take off from a student's hesitant contribution and magisterially to elaborate an extended insight from it. Instead he would characteristically respond to a student comment by listening carefully and then beginning quite elsewhere, only to work his way gradually and clearly back to the student's own final point, now leaving it open again for a different articulation and elaboration.

(The train was finally drawing into London. I thought again of George Eliot, arriving at her changing metropolis, then of her own metaphors of webs and networks, her simile (Middlemarch, ch. 38) of random scratches brought into apparent concentric order by the arbitrary placing of a lamp. I was, as it happens, returning from my father's funeral and all the lights fell a little different now. I put Terry's Theory away in my case, tucked the copy of Byte under my arm, and jumped on to the platform.)

*

[In its 1992 published form, this piece was followed by an outline of the Communications & Image Stduies degree programme mentioned. For a 1988 outline of that degree see elsehwre in this volume. I retain the list of reading and other resources which accompanied the piece in 1992, simply to indicate how far we might think we have come since.]

'Cybertheory': Suggested Readings & Resources (1992)

These titles are given in a pedagogically useful order of consultation.

Williams, Raymond (1961) *The Long Revolution.*
Anderson, Perry (1992) *English Questions..*
Eagleton, Terry (1990) *The Significance of Theory.*
Eagleton, Terry (1984) *The Function of Criticism.*

Young, J.Z. (1964) *A Model of the Brain.*
Hills, W. Daniel (1985) *The Connection Machine.*
Aleksander, Igor and Burnett, Piers (1987) *Thinking Machines.*
Kurzweil, Raymond (ed.) (1990) *The Age of Intelligent Machines.*
Lycan, William G. (ed.) (1990) *Mind and Cognition.*
Boden, Margaret (1990) *The Creative Mind.*
Davalo, Eric and Nairn, Patrick (1991) *Neural Networks.*
Dennett, Daniel C. (1992) *Consciousness Explained.*
Rucker, Rudy (1987) *Mind Tools,.*

Rucker, Rudy (1989) *Wetware.*
Gibson, William (1984) *Neuromancer.*
Gibson, William (1986) *Burning Chrome.*
Gibson, William (1986) *Count Zero.*
Gibson, William (1988) *Mono Lisa Overdrive.*
Gibson, William, Sterling, Bruce (1992) *The Difference Engine.*

Carruthers, Mary (1990) *The Book of Memory.*
Eisenstein, E. (1979) *The Printing Press as an Agent of Change.*
Brand, Stewart (1988) *The Media Lab.*
Nielsen, Jakob (1990) *Hypertext and Hypermedia.*
Rheingold, Howard (1991) *Virtual Reality.*
Benedikt, Michael (ed.) (1991) *Cyberspace.*
Hayward, Philip (ed.) (1990) *Culture, Technology and Creativity.*
Ross, Andrew (1991) *Strange Weather.*

Kinder, Marsha (1991) *Playing with Power.*
Guy Wright (1991) *Amiga Desktop Video Power.*
Philip Gladwin (1992) 'Build a brain' parts 1, 2, and 3. in *Amiga Shopper*, 14,15,16.

Ike Achebe *The Waste Land : hypertext disc* (Coventry University).

Oxford University Computing Service 'Text archive' (ARCHIVE-(SUK.AC.OXFORD.VAX).
CTI Centre for Textual Studies 'Resources guide' (CTITEXT@UK-.AC.OX.VAX).

*

COMMUNICATIONS AND IMAGE STUDIES
notes after Raymond Williams

> Checking the latest [*OED*] *Supplement* for the
> generalizing contemporary use of 'communications',
> I found an example and a date which happened to be
> from one of my own articles.[1]

Raymond Williams recounts this, wryly, to make a specific
point about the necessary limitation of any precise record of
linguistic change, his own awareness of previous possible
citations and of earlier conversational usage as evidence and
witness of that limitation. But the anecdote also encapsulates
several other familiar facets of communications and of
language: our dual relation and role, as both agents and
recipients within a circuit or network, and the dual aspect of
such systems as themselves both given and made. In our
relation to language we are both authoritatively addressed,
put in place, yet ourselves inescapably authorizers, bearing at
least partial responsibility for our own speech, whatever the
complexities of feedback, indirection and relay.

In a wider emphasis, this circuit of contribution and
return, of dual positioning and detour, could invoke that
range of social analyses which once drew their models from
linguistic exchange and interpellation. But insofar as such
emphases on structure and system shaded into a social
determinism, Williams' own emphases, across his work,
characteristically refused to follow them. Specifically, in his
work on communications, he declined to locate the 'media'
as mere mediation between levels in any base-superstructure
hierarchy; refused to align himself either with notions of
technological inevitability or with the premises of culturalist
idealism. Instead, Williams persistently offered
'communication' as both an alternative focus for
conceptualizing the social (though not itself a substitute for
that overall analysis) and as always a precondition within any
practice, not a distanced arena for 'intervention' but an
everyday possibility of empowering.

---

[1] Raymond Williams, *Keywords* (London, 1976), p. 17.

In these inquiries, as elsewhere, Williams firmly distinguished terms of analysis from terms of substance, aware that useful abstractions of method and theory, of definition and distinction, could be offered too easily as actual determinants, reified and then, apparently, even dominating. Against Saussurean-derived models, Williams preferred the road from Vitebsk: Volosinov's notions of multi-accentuality and inflection, Bakhtin's dialogicality and situatedness.[2] His own persistent bending of keywords, in his characteristically insistent inflections, both registered the necessary resistance of words and yet reconfirmed, against several kinds of denial, the shared capacity to recreate meaning from even the most familiar terms. His idiosyncratically accented vocabulary was developed as both individual engagement and as public extension, offered to others. Even if not accurate, it was then wholly appropriate that the *OED* should credit him with a decisive extension of this word, above all: 'communications'.

Other key terms in Williams' vocabulary (decidedly a vocabulary and not a terminology) also moved in several registers, often across antithetical directions of meaning. His plays take shape from layered phrases: 'making a connection', 'points of order', 'working to rule'—running a railway and conducting an investigation, two processes of network and of choice, converging in a fully political *Public Inquiry*. A 'correspondent', in *Letter from the Country*, can send private letters to public figures or patrol the parliamentary lobbies, as matters of 'public interest' are kept from an interested public.[3] Key terms, in *Culture and Society*, can be historically re-constructed in their tensely shifting senses. Crucially, as in *Marxism and Literature*, the double sense of 'determination' can hold both determinism and decision in relation, taking both stresses. For Williams, it seemed, it was often the disturbance registered in the tensions of meaning

[2] Raymond Williams, 'The Road from Vitebsk: The Uses of Cultural Theory', *New Left Review*, 158 (July-August 1986), 19-31; R. Williams, *Marxism and Literature* (Oxford, 1977), chapter 2.

[3] I have discussed Williams' plays in more detail in my contribution to *Raymond Williams: A Critical Reader*, edited by Terry Eagleton (Oxford, 1989).

across such terms that could prompt and enable articulation and understanding, a new inflection, a patient but persistent reshaping of language.[4] The first proposal in *Communications* was the old adult education priority, to teach the confidence of such (self-)transforming speech.[5] 'Communication', like 'determination', held its senses across both network and agency, the economic and the dialogical, the fully extended domain and the most immediate response: in such dual terms Williams tried to think beyond the impasses of received Marxism.

Some of Williams' specific work in 'communications', in that now explicit and general sense, could be followed and extended with a relative simplicity of method and theory, though only by a sustained labour of analysis and of forms of attention that remain rare. The several accounts, scattered through his writings, of the histories of the press or film or television; the statistical breakdowns of newspaper content or the comparative commentary on television channels; the analysis of changing patterns of prose or of forms of dramatic monologue and dialogue, within several 'media': these had been, once, exemplary and have been emulated and extended.[6] Less easy to follow has been the fertility in

---

[4] R. Williams, *Politics and Letters: Interviews with New Left Review* (London, 1979), pp. 167-8.
[5] R. Williams, *Communications* [1962] (Harmondsworth, 1976), p. 141.
[6] E.g. 'The Growth of the Popular Press', in *The Long Revolution* (London, 1961), pt 2, chapter 3;' Advertising: The Magic System', *New Left Review*, 4 (July-August 1960) and in *Problems in Materialism and Culture* (London, 1980); 'General Profile', in *Your Sunday Paper*, edited by Richard Hoggart (London, 1967); 'Radical and/or Respectable', in *The Press We Deserve*, edited by Richard Boston (London, 1970); 'The Press We Don't Deserve', in *The British Press: A Manifesto* (London, 1978); 'The Press and Popular Culture: An Historical Perspective', in *Newspaper History*, edited by George Boyce et al. (London, 1978); 'British Film History: New Perspectives', in *British Cinema History*, edited by James Curran and Vincent Porter (London, 1983); 'The Growth and Role of the Mass Media', in *Media, Politics & Culture: A Socialist View* (London, 1979), edited by Carl Gardner; 'Notes on English Prose 1780-1950', and 'On Dramatic Dialogue and Monologue' both in *Writing*

procedures and terms of analysis, the forging of usable distinctions, the directions offered for inquiry: 'drama in performance', 'structures of feeling', 'residual, dominant and emergent', 'dramatised society'. Williams' modes and phrases often became absorbed into the groundbase of others' investigations, where later methodological refinements and theoretical breaks have often seemed, by comparison, too quickly recuperable as merely items in a repertoire. Even more difficult to match, with any consistency, has been Williams' capacity for practicable proposals, for implementable institutional and political as well as pedagogical innovation.

Yet even beyond these, what was always most difficult to focus, let alone to build from, was Williams' own double relation to both the overtly 'sociological' material he dealt in and the critical inquiry he conducted. Not only the range, the movement from content-analysis to responsive judgement, as in —for example —the unusual continuities between percentage tables and ironic commentaries on a specific evening's viewing in *Communications*,[7] or the characteristic movement from concisely reconsidered history to detailed analysis to outline alternatives within a single work, as in *Television*[8] but above all the sense of an

---

in Society (London, 1984). Cf. also 'Communications as Cultural Science' in *Approaches to Popular Culture*, edited by C. W. E. Bigsby (London, 1976) and R.Williams (ed.), *Contact: Human Communication and Its Culture* (London, 1981). Williams also contributed a regular monthly column of television criticism to *The Listener* from August 1968 to January 1974. For a useful survey of the development of media studies in Britain cf. Manuel Alvarado, Robin Gutch and Tana Wollen, *Learning the Media* (London, 1987), pp. 9-39. Cf. also 'Pedagogy: Critical Accounts of Media Education', *Screen*, vol. 27, no. s (September-October 1986); *Culture, Society and the Media*, edited by M. Gurevitch et al. (London, 1982); *Media, Culture & Society: A Critical Reader*, edited by Richard Collins, et al. (London, 1986).

[7] *Communications*, pp. 90-1.

[8] *Television: Technology and Cultural Form* (London, 1974).

investigation turned back upon, and including, his own relation to and within that field of inquiry. This was not solely a matter of tone, or an autobiographical reference or two, or even the ruminatingly personal prefaces and reflections; nor, only, the often-justified sense of the appropriation of a field as if by right of personal discovery (who else, after all, could claim to have occupied some of those precise spaces before him?—hence what seemed a necessary formal innovativeness in the very organization of, for example, *The Long Revolution*, or *Modern Tragedy*, or *Towards 2000*). What came through, repeatedly, was an awareness of Williams as actively defining his own relation to an issue in the very process of constituting that issue as a matter for shared and public investigation, a determining in several senses at once. In offering, for example, a useful naming of kinds of cultural 'contributor' ('the creative artist, the performer, the reporter, the commentator') Williams immediately, though not explicitly, both provides a place for his own contributions even as he writes and yet in that writing also produces a position beyond those very categories offered. Think of this passage, in a book entitled *Communications*:

> In ordinary living, and in his [*sic*] work, the contributor shares in the life of his society, which often affects him both in minor ways and in ways sometimes so deep that he is not even aware of them. His ability to make his work public depends on the actual communication system: the language itself, or certain visual or musical or scientific conventions and the institutions through which the communication will be passed. The effect of these on his actual work can be almost infinitely variable. For it is not only a communication system outside him; it is also, however original he may be, a communication system which is in fact part of himself. Many contributors make active use of this kind of internal communication system. It is to themselves, in a way, that they first show their conceptions, play their music, present their arguments. Not only as a way of

getting these clear, in the process of almost endless testing that active composition involves. But also, whether consciously or not, as a way of putting the experience into a communicable form. If one mind has grasped it, even if only the mind that also created it, then it may be open to other minds. In this deep sense, the society is in some ways already present in the act of composition.[9]

Williams's detective-thriller novel, *The Volunteers* (1978) is, formally, the (unexpected) contribution of 'the creative artist'; but it continues these issues, centring on a reporter and several kinds of 'performer', a 'private eye' investigation that ends in a public inquiry in dramatic session. The reporter, working (already in 1978, anticipating some way into a future) for 'Insatel', global news organization, as 'consultant analyst' on the political underground, pursues a story of an 'assassination attempt' that unravels itself into a precisely planned piece of guerrilla theatre, itself only a masquerade to unmask a peculiarly impenetrable network of (counter-)penetration: the 'Volunteers' of the title are, apparently, an affiliation of oppositional 'sleepers' so profoundly camouflaged and so patiently abiding their time within the power elites that the distinction between 'them' and 'us', in any register, is perhaps no longer traceable, even to themselves (or us). A wry parable indeed. In being allowed to uncover the plot (a pre-scripted role), the reporter inevitably becomes potential informer upon his informants; yet making public their information about the Volunteers seems to be, strategically, one plausible motive for enabling him to follow the leads in the first place: to induce several layerings of confused suspicion, of anxious bluff and counter-bluff, in those very corridors of power. In finally making public an Official Secret (a 'Cabinet decision', itself on this occasion an endorsement of political murder), the reporter finds his choice to do so the only option left him: a deeply determined decision, as both intention and

---

[9] *Communications*, pp. 125—6.

imposition, insistence and initiative, a being volunteered:

> I went on staring at him. I was past assessment; past
> trying to understand him. The line between observer
> and participant, that I'd always theorized, had been
> turned so effortlessly . . . And right in the middle of
> this shared and satisfying voluntary act I was turned,
> without hesitation, into another and much more
> difficult action. And not by his force, as he said. By
> my own momentum. By my own style.[10]

Later, as the decisive action is being taken:

> To be there and to be telling it was a local moment, a
> significant moment, but the immense process
> continued and there was no available identity outside
> it: only the process itself, which could never be
> properly told in any single dimension or any single
> place. There was only, now, the deep need to connect
> and the practical impossibility, for unregrettable
> reasons, of making the connections, even the known
> connections. Yet then, all the time, within this
> impossibility, were the inevitable commitments, the
> necessary commitments, the choosing of sides.
> Through the persistent uncertainty, within the
> overwhelming process, I had now chosen and been
> chosen, in what would be, in effect, a quite final way.[11]

What is here defined and explored, in both analysis and
imagination, is a deep structure of feeling—as always, an
intimate interlocking of process and pressure, but now,
within our contemporary relations of communication and
power, harder even than usual to grasp, since the very
divisions we have relied on to establish the space for analysis
are themselves transformed as an effect of those same
pressures: the privilege of perspective becomes the instant

---

[10] *The Volunteers* (London, 1978), p. 179.
[11] *Ibid.* p. 207.

commentator's assumed viewpoint, the effort at fuller comprehension now the received ritual of 'balance'.[12] Again, Williams locates in the novel a moment of disturbance, even in the practised professional witness (the on-the-spot reporter now on the spot):

> I walked to the witness stand. I was moving automatically but some emotion was running through me that I could not understand, could not even recognize. I say emotion but that is too abstract. It was a physical condition: as of an intense otherness, an intense possession by otherness. My ordinary self seemed no more than a bearer: a physical attendance, upon some other being and event . . .
> Then the physical relations changed. There was Counsel for the Union: a man on his feet, a man speaking to me, and the others were fading.[13]

Elsewhere, Williams locates these themes of dissociation and distantiation in a wider pattern—in his 1974 inaugural lecture as, precisely, Professor of Drama:

> we have never as a society acted so much or watched so many others acting . . . for the first time a majority of the population has regular and constant access to drama, beyond occasion or season . . . drama, in quite new ways, is built into the rhythms of everyday life. On television alone it is normal for viewers—the substantial majority of the population to see anything up to three hours of drama, of course drama of several different kinds, a day. And not just one day; almost every day. This is part of what I mean by a

---

[12] Cf. the remark in *Marxism and Literature*, p. n : 'When the most basic concepts —the concepts, as it is said, from which we begin — are suddenly seen to be not concepts but problems, not analytic problems either but historical movements that are still unresolved, there is no sense in listening to their sonorous summons or their resounding clashes. We have only, if we can, to recover the substance from which their forms were cast.'

[13] *The Volunteers*, p. 199.

dramatised society . . . What we now have is drama as habitual experience: more in a week, in many cases, than most human beings would previously have seen in a lifetime . . . To watch simulated action, of several recurrent kinds, not just occasionally but regularly, for longer than eating and for up to half as long as work or sleep; this, in our kind of society, as majority behaviour, is indeed a new form and pressure.[14]

The specific conventions of this particular dramatisation . . are not abstract. They are profoundly worked and re-worked in our actual living relationships. They are our ways of seeing and knowing, which every day we put into practice, and while the conventions hold, while the relationships hold, most practice confirms them. One kind of specific autonomy—this-ness, here-ness—is in part free of them; but this is usually an autonomy of privacy, and the private figure—the character of the self—is already widely offered to be appropriated in one or other of these dramatised forms.[15]

In this dramatized society, arguably, the crucial modulation within the structure of feeling has been a deep convolution precisely of feeling, a kind of dualism or doubling within the structure of feeling itself: an awareness simultaneously of dramatizing our feelings and of faking even the dramatization, no longer simply role-playing or pre-scribed reactions but an over-laying so complete and involuted that the distinctions between dramatized feeling and actual response, between enabling convention and merely residual code, become finally un-decidable, in-decipherable.

In his novel, *Loyalties* (1985), Williams gives a rich treatment to—among others—precisely this issue. The framing device of the novel, an investigation by a television

---

[14] *Drama in a Dramatised Society* (Cambridge, 1975), pp. 4-5. A version of the lecture is also included in *Writing in Society*, pp. 11-21.
[15] *Drama in a Dramatised Society*, pp. 15-16.

researcher into yet more allegations of old espionage (Williams, we recall, was nearly of that notorious Cambridge generation), includes moments of indecipherability, an inscrutability of feeling and reaction:

> Allicon was staring into Jon's face as he spoke. Then he looked away, smiling sadly.
> 'Actors, Jon, I understand. I say, darling—anguish. Darling—passion, confusion, curiosity, blissful contentment. And the thing is, you see, they then do it. Can do it. Amateurs on the other hand do not. Cannot. Though doubtless they have one or another—who knows which?—of those emotions.'[16]

And, later, in the symptomatic enthusiasm for a new TV series, on the radicals and romantics of the 1790s, the issue of dramatization is touched again:

> 'It would be difficult to do,' Jon said, again carefully.
> 'I'm talking about a series, Jon. A dramatic series.'
> 'Based on those lives?'
> 'On the intercut of those lives. The people and the politics. The sad and muddled passions of our own time at once foreshadowed and projected in these legendary figures. At once life and larger than life . . . . Here, in our own history, is a story running over with causes and excitements, passions and sensations, beyond anything these pallid suburbans could concoct. Phil saw the possibilities at once.'
> 'You mean this is the new project? '
> 'It is. He's lining it up. And as a big co-production. Eight, perhaps ten.'
> 'With actors?'
> 'With actors.'

---

[16] *Loyalties* (London, 1985), p. 374.

'Darling, anguish. Darling, a cause?'[17]

The synthetic accents of this simulated speech are caught with sufficient precision to make us doubtful how to judge the writing itself: a further layering of undecidability.

Taken together, as Williams' own extension of his work on communications, *Drama in a Dramatised Society*, *Volunteers* and *Loyalties* can suggest a complex consonance between, say, the world of *Smiley's People* and that of Baudrillard's *Simulations*, a terrain for which several preliminary sketch-maps have already been provided, from Daniel Boorstin's 'guide to pseudo-events' *(The Image*, 1961) to Debord's cartography of the *Society of the Spectacle* (1967) but which now invites a fuller exploration. Williams' own mode of engagement, however, was neither that of exempt expert nor that of ironic spectator or voyeur, but that of reflexive inhabitant. If we need a name for this field of reflexive inquiry we can label it pragmatically, provisionally, as distinguishable from 'communications' yet, like 'communications', both a focus for reconceptualizing the social and as indicating a decisive extension, in practice, of the objects and forms now needing to be understood. As a working label, 'Image Studies' will do.

The generalizing, encompassing extension, in another area, from 'Literature' to 'text' to 'writing' can be paralleled: 'image' can not only cover the fields of both those currently impassed disciplines, film studies and art history, but can extend considerably beyond either. But its usefulness lies primarily in its ambivalence, its dual sense of both representation and mis-representation, both reliable appearance of a real and mere chimera, both reflection and fiction, as counterpart to, and constituent of, that doubled structure of feeling. To think of 'image(s)' as a focus, to foreground our reflexive relation (images from imaging) to this now extended provision—profusion, proliferation, permeation—of processes of imaging, is to shift even further from any still residual model of merely linear or

---

[17] *Ibid.*, p. 376

reciprocal transmission of messages as a known mode of 'communication', with the distancing dispersal of roles and formal distribution of functions comfortingly appropriate to such models, and to recognize not only the increased importance of specifiable images (visuals) within 'communications' but also the increased realization of a peculiarly mirroring relation between appearances, including one's own: almost a dissolution of distinctions between the reflexive and the fictive.

IMAGE PILGRIMS

I stand with my 6-year-old daughter, looking through a set of railings across the entombed effigy of the Black Prince; on the far side, a line of kneeling figures, white-shawled, hands clasped in devotion. Glimmering before them in gold, a shrine, candles lit. The guardian of the shrine, dimmed shape in darkness, intones prayers and admonitions. We shuffle past, down the stone passage, and into the jostling group in the market-place: sellers' cries and buyers' queries; a pottery stall, a fishwife, a street-trader in trinkets, badges, souvenirs. We wander on, through open double doors, into a large bright shop, selling trinkets, badges, souvenirs: pilgrims' badges, books of hours, illuminated gospels —the Heritage Shop at the exit from the Canterbury Pilgrims Way. We have come through a medieval environment, complete with smells, constructed within a medieval church, have seen and heard presentations of five of Chaucer's tales of pilgrimage, and now we buy the illustrated brochure of our own 'journey'.[18]

A step into the high street. Over the road, down Mercery Lane, the great Christ Church gate of the cathedral is visible. To our left, a queue outside a one-hour photo-developing service; three chain stores selling TVs, video-recorders, camcorders; three commercial art galleries; the Beaney Museum; the Sidney Cooper Centre, now an indoor market (Cooper, 'Britain's most accomplished cattle painter'); and in the near distance the Westgate Towers, now also a museum. To our right, a pavement artist with recognizable masterpieces in chalk, and another offering portraits to passers-by ; a poster shop; a Roman pavement on view; a cinema; and beyond the roundabout (its subways covered with murals of Canterbury Tales, themselves covered with graffiti), an art

---

[18] For a brief account of the Canterbury Pilgrims Way Centre see Jennifer Uglow, 'Back Projections', *TLS*, 12 August 1988.

college. Everywhere, tourists taking photos.

We join them (entering their viewfinders) before the cathedral gate: imposing, impressive, photogenic. The twin towers of the west facade of the cathedral itself are even more photogenic; or the south-west porch, taking the shot upwards to Bell Harry tower. Unmistakable images. Unforgettable. Recordable. Within the cathedral, we stand looking down upon the spot of Becket's martyrdom, murder, celebrity. Beyond, dim in a corner, a tomb effigy, simple, wooden, bare, of Archbishop Pecham (d. 1292). To our right, another tomb effigy. Archbishop Chichele (d. 1443), a double effigy, berobed and —below—'gisant' cadaver, the whole monument enframed by miniature towers and turrets, bristling with bright-painted figures, shields, emblems. Between us and Chichele, two 'Bible windows', stained-glass resplendent, 'Biblia Pauperum' arrangements in vivid colour, complex patternings of type and ante-type. Next to them, a palely painted wall, the Life of St Eustace, layered narrative. Beyond Chichele, the 'miracle windows', medallions of homage, tales of devotion. Before us, pale lights and rich colours, the north-west transept window. Behind us, magnificent, the great south window.

But: the south window was entirely rebuilt in 1792, and most of the glass is relocated from elsewhere. Of the north window, 'only the royal portraits and the angels holding shields escaped destruction during the Puritan onslaught in 1643; these remnants were rearranged' around 1774 (Rackham).[19] The first miracle window 'has always retained its original-border. The remainder is made up partly of scraps of ancient glass . . partly of modern glass'; 'five of the medallions . . . belonged to . . . other windows in the series' (Rackham). The St. Eustace wall-painting was barely traceable ten years ago; its present impact comes from extensive restoration. In the Bible windows 'the panels have become somewhat muddled, and the aim of the whole scheme, as a theological commentary, has thus become confused' (Ingram Hill). Chichele's tomb was 'thoroughly

---

[19] Information on the cathedral is drawn from Bernard Rackham, *The Stained Glass Windows of Canterbury Cathedral* (Canterbury, 1957); D. Ingrain Hill, *Canterbury Cathedral* (London, 1986); Jonathan Keates and Angelo Hornak, *Canterbury Cathedral* (London, 1987).

restored' in 1897; the statues and heraldry are all Victorian. The photogenic clutter of niche-figures in the south-west porch dates from the 1860s, by Pfyffers, mediocre Belgian sculptor. The memorably symmetrical west facade dates only from the demolition of the north-west Norman tower in 1832 and its replacement by a copy of Mapillon's fifteenth-century south-west bell-tower. And Christ Church Gate 'owes much to a great restoration begun in 1931 . . . the twin turrets which are now a prominent feature of the design were demolished in 1803 and replaced by careful replicas in 1937' (Ingram Hill).

This isn't, of course, the whole (familiar) story of our modern pilgrimage, but the videos and snapshots which carefully frame the twin turrets of the great gateway or capture the symmetrical towers of the west facade are recording images of replicas, constructed appearances, only less apparently so than the life-size models and sets in the Heritage industry's Pilgrims Way. And, of course, the cathedral shop sells almost identical souvenirs to that Heritage shop: facsimiles, reproductions, replicas, miniature versions of stained glass, brasses, medallions, bosses, badges. Two and a half million tourists visited the cathedral last season.

Layered upon each other in this short stroll from St Margaret's ex-church to the re-restored cathedral are several distinct scopic regimes and visual logics, now subsumed into and transformed by the present image economy: a palimpsest of past imagings and uses of images, now seen, looked at, predominantly if not exclusively, as potential mental souvenirs, as camera material, as memorable 'sights'. It is possible, though with genuine difficulty, to attend differently to this assemblage of imagings, against the grain of tourist consumption and appreciation. It would be possible, for example, to trace several instructive but dispersed historical routes, from Roman Pavement to pavement artists, from Chichele's *gisant* to Chaucerian make-believes, from Pecham's science of optics[20] to the Athena poster shop, from Chichele's arguments with the later Lollards[21] to the Heritage display of audio-visual aids, from Puritan iconoclasm[22] to modern-day pilgrimage.[23] Such trajectories might be tracked as an exercise in an extended version of art history, or as an inquiry into the relation of images to power in different forms of social control and communication, or as a more open investigation into the functioning of images within historically changing apparatuses, institutions, social and discursive formations.

What seems, however, to have emerged in the recent kaleidoscope of research and theory is a recognition of another object of analysis, in some ways akin to Foucault's notion of *'épistème'*. The terms tentatively employed earlier — image economy, scopic regime, visual logic—provisionally indicate this conceptual focus, though as yet only a range of

---

[20] David C. Lindberg, *John Pecham and the Science of Optics* (University of Wisconsin Press, 1970) includes an edition of Pecham's *Perspectiva communis*, which had become the standard text on optics by the fourteenth century and remained so into the seventeenth.

[21] Cf. Margaret Aston, *Lollards and Reformers: Images and Literacy in Late Medieval Religion* (London, 1984), pp. 29-30, 78-81, 85-6. It was while Archbishop Courtenay (whose tomb is also in the cathedral) was attending the Blackfriars Council against the Wycliffites in 1382 that an earthquake destroyed the cathedral bell-tower, necessitating the construction of the present south-west bell-tower. One wonders how either archbishop would react, for example, to the use, since the St Bartholomew Day exodus of French Calvinists, of part of the crypt as a Huguenot chapel.

[22] Cf. e.g. John Phillips, *The Reformation of Images: Destruction of Art in England, 1535-1660* (University of California Press, 1973), pp. 189-94. The classic contemporary account is by the participant-observer Richard Culmer, *Cathedrall Newes from Canterbury* (London, 1644).

[23] J. G. Davies, *Pilgrimage Yesterday and Today* (London, 1988), pp. 152-60, gives an account of the surprisingly recent revival of pilgrimages to Canterbury. Cf. also Victor Turner and Edith.Turner, *Image and Pilgrimage in Christian Culture* (New York, 1978).

rather disparate and perhaps incompatible inquiries can be claimed as contributions to the emergent defining of this formal object. For example, Foucault's own work on the clinical gaze, or Bryson's essay on the logic of the gaze in/as the history of art; de Certeau's analysis of Nicolas of Cusa's *De Icona* or John Barrell's account of the eighteenth-century spectatorial stance; the work of Debord and Baudrillard, of Haug and Mitchell would all figure in any brief bibliography of the field.[24]

Despite the obvious disparities, it is perhaps now becoming possible to sketch not just single-strand trajectories or periodizations of a 'style', but a preliminary typology of overall image economies in their relation to visual logics and scopic regimes, each most manifestly occupying but not restricted to a relatively specific historical

---

[24] The references are familiar: M. Foucault, *The Birth of the Clinic* (London, 1973), *Discipline and Punish* (London, 1977), 'The Eye of Power', in *Power/Knowledge* edited by Colin Gordon (Brighton, 1980); cf. also Martin Jay, 'In the Empire of the Gaze', in *Postmodernism: ICA Documents* 4 (London, 1986), and John Rajchman, 'Foucault's Art of Seeing', *October* 44 (spring 1988); G. Deleuze, in *Foucault* (Paris, 1986), uses the term *visibilités* but this hasn't yet, I think, been acclimatized into English; Norman Bryson, *Vision and Painting: The Logic of the Gaze* (London, 1983); Michel de Certeau, 'The Gaze: Nicholas of Cusa', *Diacritics* vol. 17, no. 3 (fall 1987); John Barrell, *An Equal Wide Survey* (London, 1983); Guy Debord, *Society of the Spectacle* (Detroit, 1970); Jean Baudrillard, *Simulations* (New York, 1983), *The Ecstasy of Communication* (New York, 1988), *The Evil Demon of Images* (Sydney, 1987); Wolfgang Haug, *Critique of Commodity Aesthetics: Appearance, Sexuality and Advertising in Capitalist Society* (Cambridge, 1986); W. J. T. Mitchell, *Iconology: Image, Text, Ideology* (Chicago, 1986) and *The Language of Images*, edited by W. J. T. Mitchell (Chicago, 1980). My own preferred terms overlap with but are not intended to be identical with the specific terminology of any of these writers. An adequate comparison and critique is well beyond the scope of this brief essay and would certainly have to include, for example, Barthes, *Image/Music/Text*, and Irigaray, *Speculum*, as well as some recent attempts at synthesis or overview: Richard Kearney, *The Wake of Imagination* (London, 1988), and David M. Levin, *The Opening of Vision* (New York, 1988).

moment and each constituted by internal relations between designated 'objects' and characteristic 'modes' of vision, of visibility and visualization, realized as specific practices, institutions and apparatuses—including but not confined to those of the various systems of 'communications'.

An imprecise, provisional schema can fairly easily be outlined, with the offered terminology left at present relatively undefined. At the most basic, we might speak of physiological processes of perception as entailing a primary logic of *registration* and *recognition,* formally distinct from a logic of *remembrance* and both incorporated into and contributing to a logic of *imagining.* Taken together, these distinguishable components of a foundational regime of perception comprise roughly the field of problems which preoccupied Freud, for example, in the 1895 *Project* and in chapter 7 of *The Interpretation of Dreams*; Lacan's work on the mirror phase and the Imaginary also has its primary reference here.[25]

A regime of *realization* might then be discriminated, as including, for example, two distinct modes of *display,* in the erotic and in the realm of power: the spectacle as exhibition and as demonstration.[26] A regime of *revelation* (concealment, un-veiling, *a-letheia,* truth) might be distinguished, for example, into the modes of icon and of vision, of a gaze directed at us from the plane of truth (the eyes of the 'Eastern' icon, its inverse perspective), as against the

---

[25] This is not to suggest that either Freud's or Lacan's notions are to be thought of without historical or cultural specificity. Lacan attempts to clarify the relation between 'the Gaze' and the history of both optics and painting in *The Four Fundamental Concepts of Psycho-Analysis* (London, 1977), chapters 6-9.

[26] Analysis of both forms in the Renaissance period might begin from, e.g. Roy Strong, *Art and Power: Renaissance Festivals 1450-1650* (Woodbridge, 1984), and Ioan P. Couliano, *Eros and Magic in the Renaissance* (Chicago, 1987). Roland Barthes, *Sade/Fourier /Loyola* (New York, 1976), provides a still undeveloped basis for a wider analysis. Cf. also Jacqueline Rose, *Sexuality in the Field of Vision* (London, 1987).

('Western') window upon the divine, an opening through which we peer and perhaps penetrate (the stained glass of Canterbury, the heavenly ceilings of the Renaissance).[27] Both the regimes of realization and of revelation may be subsumed under a more comprehensive logic, that of the Glimpse: the elusively incomplete, though not necessarily fleeting, character of the visibility of the divine, of power, even of the sexual.

A different overall logic, that of the Gaze, might include several distinguishable (and familiar) regimes: that of *representation*, a relatively secularized regime of appearances, and especially of forms of 'realism'; that of *reproduction*, the arena of the artefact as explicitly artificial, a matter of artifice; that of the *spectatorial* (in which, for example, an actual rather than a represented landscape is received as a view but no longer as a vision).

A logic of the Scan might be designated, as including regimes of *surveillance* and *supervision*, of *oversight* and *inspection* (the various territories of Foucault's panopticon, prison, clinic, but more generally of scientific objectivity and organized detachment). Interrelated with and perhaps connecting both these logics are the claims of the aesthetic (scrutiny as 'pure' gaze, another detachment) and modes of imitation (as modelling and approximation or aspiration, in 'art', in knowledge-construction and in, for example, the pleasures of costume, of fashionable replay, of display returned as social theatre, as in the several 'Camelot'

---

[27] For the theology underpinning the Eastern icon cf. e.g. Leonid Ouspensky, *Theology of the Icon* (London, 1978), Vladimir Lossky, *In the Image and Likeness of God* (London, 1974), chapter 7, and *The Mystical Theology of the Eastern Church* (London, 1957), chapter 6; cf. also John Baggley, *Doors of Perception* (Oxford, 1987). For an account of the Western theology and iconography of the door cf. e.g. Titus Burckhardt, *Sacred Art in East and West* (Bedfont, 1976), chapter 3, and the classic account of the tympanum and porch of Moissac in Meyer Schapiro, *Romanesque Art* (London, 1977). The sense of an opening in the wall into an imagined sacred space can of course be traced back at least to Roman mural painting, cf. Gilbert Picard, *Roman Painting* (New York, 1968), chapter 2.

moments of English ruling class self-presentation).[28]

A logic different from those of perception, of glimpse and of gaze, seems to be at work in the current dominant regime of (as a general term) *recording*, which clearly incorporates both a new modulation of the spectacular and the (re-)emergence of simulation. The overall logic here is that of the Glance: a rapidation of registration and recognition, to the point where any promise of gaze or expectation of glimpse, any anticipation of aesthetic pleasure or hope of religious revelation, or even any prospect of stabilized understanding, is permanently postponed, while still apparently motivating response and reaction: a perpetual procrastination (rather than look long at a landscape, we take photos for a future scrutiny that never arises), or a simple evacuation of one instant image by another (a permanent condition of news-ness).

Clearly, these tentative and disposable terms merely designate areas of analysis already partly explored. They might, for example, be taken as mapping a discernible anthropological-historical trajectory, from the primitivism of erotic display to the modes of metropolitan post-modernism. This would be one possible development and direction for inquiry. But in labelling the overall object of analysis 'image economies' I intend to suggest rather that the relation of these various regimes (themselves terms of analysis rather than terms of substance) is not simply that of succession or precession, but of potential co-existence, or incorporation within a dominantly structured combinatory.

For example, the regime of representation may well seek to re-present the artefacts, the material images, produced within the earlier dominance of another regime, that of, say, revelation (any museum already exemplifies this, the tourist-orientation of Canterbury Cathedral partly acknowledges it).[29] Or the regime of recording may re-deploy both the

---

[28] Cf. Mark Girouard, *The Return to Camelot* (New Haven, 1981).

[29] For example, the entries on religious objects in *The Medieval Treasury*, edited by Paul Williamson for the Victoria and Albert Museum (1986), tell us almost nothing of their liturgical or devotional use but include, as in an art auction catalogue, detailed

spectatorial mode and its preferred images (the picturesque panning shots of wide landscapes in various filmic systems). Equally, and alternatively, certain regimes may be wholly unable to incorporate either the material or the modes of earlier regimes: the result can be hostility (as in the several moments of iconoclasm, of one regime rejecting and destroying the favoured objects of another),[30] or of incomprehension (as in our own incapacity to understand, let alone reproduce, the dream-disciplines of Asclepius or of Aborigines, or our bafflement at beliefs in the magic powers of images).[31]

These possible relations between regimes—partial (mis-) appropriation, negation and exclusion, incomprehension or indifference—might well be elaborated and refined, along lines similar to Foucault's original exploration of shifts in epistemic logics yet also, perhaps, in terms of Williams' cultural materialist emphases. It may even be more feasible than in Foucault's case to attempt to relate the modulations within and between scopic regimes, or even overall image economies, to more permanent structures and restraints of perception: the relation between the apparent analog character of sight and the digital mechanism of retinal reception may, for example, perpetually generate the several systems of framing and focusing which could also, as repeated procedures of image organization, be mapped onto

---

discussion of their provenance and craftsmanship (e.g. the entry oh a 'Devotional Booklet', p. 212, leaves wholly unexplained the use in meditation of the images illustrated). Similarly, the many entries on Canterbury stained glass in John Barker, *English Stained Glass* (London, 1978) tell us nothing of their religious meaning. Contrast the exemplary explanatory commentary in the facsimile edition of the *Biblia Pauperum* by Avril Henry (Aldershot, 1987).

[30] Cf. e.g. Peter Brown, 'A Dark Age Crisis: Aspects of the Iconoclastic Controversy', in his *Society and the Holy in Late Antiquity* (London, 1982), and Carlos M. N. Eire, *War Against the Idols: The Reformation of Worship from Erasmus to Calvin* (Cambridge, 1986).

[31] On the incubation chambers ofAsclepius and related practices cf. Robin Lane Fox, *Pagans and Christians* (Harmondsworth, 1988), chapter 4: 'Seeing the Gods'.

the various regimes. A complex set of factors structuring any specific regime or economy could be analysed along such lines. That would be another feasible direction for inquiry.

Whether any such analyses would either require or constitute a new 'discipline' ('imagistics'?) or merely indicate the converging futures of several present disciplines (under the loose aegis of 'image studies') is unclear and perhaps not important. Clearly, for example, the new degree in 'Communications and Image Studies' at the University of Kent at Canterbury is constructed at present as a repertoire of several contributions rather than upon a putative theoretical synthesis or a prior methodological allegiance.[32]

Courses in Media Studies are, of course, already well established, especially in the polytechnics (see Alvarado *et al.*, note 6 above) though many of these have been oriented very firmly to current developments and, often, to the acquisition of practical skills (see, for example, the range of courses offered by Birkbeck College to adult students, from 'Community Radio' to 'Feminism and Cinema'). However, the Kent degree, perhaps like those developing at Goldsmiths and at Sussex, for example, reflects a sense that both the changes in the media themselves and in the context of education now require a much longer perspective upon contemporary developments, which is one of the reasons for the new overlaps with art history and with cultural anthropology, and also that the very success of practical media courses might now allow the emergence of a form of 'media' studies less specifically concerned with current technical possibilities.

Any overall synthesis of theory and method would indeed be difficult, though it is relatively easy to sketch a general scope or programme of possible objectives for 'image studies': to re-define and extend the material of analysis to include the widest range of 'image' (from

---

[32] An outline of the degree is available from the Humanities Admissions Office, University of Kent, Canterbury. The degree is structured round core courses taught by philosophers, art historians, social anthropologists, cultural historians and media sociologists, with optional courses drawn from film studies, drama, linguistics, psychoanalysis, art history, computing, etc. [See below]

paintings to postcards, from fantasies to films, from dreams to ads, from snaps to maps); to analyse the role of images within the several social apparatuses (in education and religion, the penal and the military)[33], and more generally the relation of image economies to forms of power; to develop a coherent formal schema of the constituent elements of regimes, logics and image economies (the combinations of stance, viewpoint, frame, object, institution, etc.); and, perhaps, to trace an overall interrelation or trajectory across the several image economies which might be historically distinguished. But, of course, the very scope of any such programme would imply considerable pedagogical difficulties. The diversity of specialisms required to track the full layerings of regimes at work even in a day out in Canterbury should be enough to indicate some of the more obvious difficulties of range and competence.

Any 'discipline' must, for teaching purposes, have a manageable inexhaustibility, that is, it must both provide, especially for students, the possibility of their own continuing search and discovery, without mere repetition and circularity, and yet also focus on a sufficiently limited amount of definite material for the student to reach some genuine coherence of understanding. Two familiar ways of achieving this general aim can be distinguished: the construction of a limited canon of material in which the material itself is regarded as inexhaustible (e.g. the alleged 'richness' and 'profundity' of selected literary texts); or the continually renewed accumulation of data, in accordance with some restricted though revisable procedures and criteria of appropriateness (the paradigm here might be the work of the historian).

Development of a comprehensive 'image studies' would seem to have difficulty in either constructing a canon of material or in embarking on any manageable accumulation:

---

[33] An urgent area for inquiry would be the convergence of military image technologies, in the use of simulation trainers, of electronic sensors and guidance-systems, of satellite surveillance, of artificial visual mapping systems, etc., particularly in relation to the 'male fantasies' of military personnel.

the very ephemerality and diversity of its possible objects seem to militate against either mode. Perhaps instead a kind of cue might be taken from Brecht: in proposing an abolition of aesthetics, a refusal of that model of profundity, and in advancing a 'historicizing' rather than accumulative notion of history, Brecht characteristically practised a form of alienation-effect, a de-mystifying making-strange, that both aimed to disclose the how and why of an event or process and to situate both performer and spectator within a shared space of experiment and modification, a relativizing of both past and present in the same gesture.[34]

At the directly pedagogical level, 'image studies'—in its own refusal of 'aesthetic' criteria or accumulative ambition —might well adopt similar alienation-effect exercises, a practical learning through, say, a deliberate mis-matching of modes and materials from distinct regimes, or a revival of older modes in relation to modern materials. One could envisage students, for example, applying the procedures of the *ars memoriae* to the making of alternative forms of advertisement, or adapting the practices of the Ignatian spiritual exercises to their comprehension of a television news-broadcast, or analysing modern personality cults (stars or Stalins) in the light of the theology of the icon. But if the overall aim is neither appreciation nor accumulation, what would be the point of such exercises, of the development of 'image studies' in the first place?

The contention would be that insofar as the object of analysis includes and, in a Brechtian historicizing sense, takes shape from, the present image economy which we inhabit and which contributes to our very constitution (our self-image, our imaginary relation to the more general social economies), then 'image studies'—like the study of language or communication in a Volosinov or Bakhtinian mode— aims primarily at a situated and enabling reflexiveness.

---

[34] Bertolt Brecht, 'Shouldn't we Abolish Aesthetics ?', in *Brecht on Theatre*, edited by John Willett (London, 1964), and 'Second Appendix", note 3, in *The Messingkauf Dialogues* (London, 1965). Cf. also, of course, Raymond Williams, *Drama from Ibsen to Brecht* (London, 1968).

Hence the example (which, itself offered as image, would need to be analysed) of the Canterbury day out.

But, of course, the boundaries of 'situation' can be variously circumscribed: in a radio talk on 'Welsh culture', for example, Williams very deliberately specified the National Coal Board and British Rail, NATO and the EEC, as constituents of 1970s 'Welsh' culture. Crucial to our present situation, our doubled structure of feeling, it might be argued, is precisely the inter-relation of 'image' and 'real', an awareness that everything, it seems, can exist twice over, as itself and as image of itself, or—increasingly—that the claim of the 'real' is put in suspension (*epoché*) leaving only an 'image' without its 'real'.

The very use of scare-quotes in that last sentence is itself an instance of this doubling across a vacancy: concepts and terms are signalled as only standing in place of, yet that which they substitute for has no other mode of availability (*traces, erasures*). More widely, the very preoccupation with theory and method in contemporary cultural studies speaks of a related doubling: of wanting to know about knowing (epistemology) precisely because we don't really know if we know (methodology). But what is then perhaps most important is the recognition that a substantially new disciplinary formation takes shape not primarily from prior theoretical elaboration or from advance methodological refinement (the familiar procrastinations of the Ph.D. student), but from a continuing practice, arising from an initial engagement of practitioners round a common, if decidedly emergent, object which seems to demand, without yet yielding, a theory and method. The opening definition, the enabling recognition, of such an object of inquiry is what allows a discipline to emerge.

Which returns us to Raymond Williams. His recognition of the 'object' which took shape in *Culture and Society* was, more than any other in Britain, the enabling moment for what became 'Cultural Studies', while that *OED* citation of his use of 'communications' signals a similar moment of redefinition, even though Williams rightly refuses the credit of any simple priority. In more specific ways, too, his work on communications may now prove exemplary for any development of 'image studies'. His various analyses of drama and the media already refused to accept the categories of the aesthetic or the procedures of formal analysis as decisive, while at the same time resisting any collapse of the specificities of form (including the 'aesthetic' effect or impact) into a simple epiphenomenon of the apparatus, of technique or technology. Characteristically, aesthetic, formal and institutional analyses were all located within a wider social analysis (itself dispersed across several kinds of writing), but that social analysis was not presented as only a detached investigation into a distanced object, but as necessarily also requiring a reflexive account—even if obliquely—of Williams' own situatedness, his position as a moment within the processes he traces (hence his implicit self-inclusion within the lineage outlined in *Culture and Society*, or his provision of a modern tragedy in *Modern Tragedy*). Any such reflexive, self-situating account could then include the specific response, the explicit formal awareness, the impact of pleasure, as the very way in which an endemically social process might be substantially registered and realized *as*, for example, 'theatre' (drama in performance) or 'television'. Williams' apparently idio-syncratic incorporation of his own 'experience' into the analysis was precisely consonant with his refusal of any simple bifurcation of the social into base and superstructure, into determining and determined. For him 'communication' provided the instantiation, as well as the exemplification, of the dual sense of 'determination'.

In the case of 'image studies' a similar refusal to prioritize the aesthetic seems required (a prising open of the categories of the regimes of representation and reproduction which have tended to motivate and justify the selective appropriation of other regimes as themselves objects of aesthetic appreciation or pleasure)—but equally a rejection of the kind of disengaged formalism which can, sophistically, reduce the entirety of the social to spectacle or to simulation (repressing even the residual recognition that, for example, 'miniaturization' destroys Asian workers' eyesight or that disasters remain devastating beyond their jaded news-worthiness). The points at which the scopic regime presently dominant in the western metropolis—that of simulation—is unavoidably encountered yet also resisted is precisely in the doubled domain of apparently 'personal experience' and feeling: that is, each of us can indeed attempt reflexively to analyse our own elusive relation to the simulations and dramatizations which constitute our own self-image(s), not as introspection but in the first instance as layered description.[35]

But then the material effectiveness of the overall social construction of the regime of simulation is quite palpably enacted through and witnessed within the 'giddiness' Baudrillard speaks of,[36] which folds the logic of the glimpse onto the logic of glance, with our 'self' as the elusively evanescent image, perpetually procrastinated. In one sense, the very difficulty of achieving a pedagogy in and of these conditions then itself becomes the exemplary instantiation of the doubleness, the element of simulacrum, which is both the object and the presupposition of the inquiry. Scopic regimes are materially realized not least in those subjected to them. Which is one reason why, in principle, work in 'image studies' could indeed begin anywhere—a day out with a daughter, a rose-window, an iconoclastic tract, a royal procession, a political demonstration, a press photo, an advert, a home video, a dream. It is not that the social *is* the image, but that one crucial constitutive of the social is the very relay of the social *as* image. It is then a condition of the inquiry that we cannot locate a space for analysis detached from that very process: again, a continuity once again with the problematic of 'communications' and with the dual facet of 'determination'.

---

[35] It is here perhaps that a specific contribution might be sought from psychoanalysis. Cf. the very different discussions of imaging in *Formations of Fantasy* edited by Victor Burgin, James Donald and Cora Kaplan (London, 1986) and in Julia Segal, *Phantasy in Everyday Life* (Harmondsworth, 1985).
[36] Jean Baudrillard, 'Forget Baudrillard', in *Forget Foucault* (New York, 1987), esp. pp. 81ff.

Williams' work—intriguingly—provided, overall, neither a theory nor a method,[37] but rather, in advancing this profoundly reflexive mode of cultural materialism (think, for example, of how *The Country and the City* can sometimes seem like a deeply historical 'auto-biography' of Williams' own location across the various cultural and social borders he traces), Williams seemed able, in that very reaction, to propose and partly construct quite new explicit 'objects' of analysis ('the long revolution', for instance, is more than a notional phrase), though at the same time often including a revised typology and a revalued history of already familiar topics and issues. Yet Williams then sought to go beyond these difficult yet preliminary enablings towards an 'operational' stance: the point of investigation and categorization was to establish ways of resisting, opposing, changing, the present patterns of power, if only because those patterns of power were constitutive of the situation from which reflection began.

If 'image studies' is to develop past the mere elaboration of schemas and histories, the refinement of terms and concepts, or even the complex analysis of specific image economies, it will not only have to confront pedagogical difficulties but also questions of political engagement. But the problems of achieving any oppositional 'bending' or counter-inflection within an image economy are curiously compounded, not only by the high degree of implication of any image economy into other social economies, or by the intrinsic polysemanticity of all images, their already multiple inflection and therefore their dependence upon (con-textual) anchorage for specificity. The crucial dilemma is the capacity of an image economy to incorporate all forms of image-making into itself, precisely insofar as the very visibility of such images is pre-scribed by that economy. There is a

---

[37] Williams' most apposite programmatic essays are probably 'Means of Communication as Means of Production' and 'Base and Superstructure in Marxist Cultural Theory', both in *Problems in Materialism and Culture*, and the highly condensed *Culture* (London, 1981).

parallel here to Brecht's lament, that bourgeois theatre could 'theatre it all down'.

It may be that the only eventual mode of opposition to a dominant image economy is always, finally, a repudiation of images, a practical iconoclasm— though all iconoclasms perhaps destroy only partial objects, selected according to the rejected protocols they seek to supersede. Image studies may be only a moment in the development of another iconoclasm: a de-realization rather than celebration of the regimes of representation, reproduction, and recording, insofar as these constitute the present image economy. But iconoclasms as well as regimes are realizable only as material practices, which is perhaps one reason why the institutional space has already been created for a discipline that yet lacks, and may never develop, a theory or a method, or even perhaps a definable object. As a discipline, 'Image Studies' may not even have a future at all, though it now has a name. That the name, as yet, designates what may remain only a simulation or simulacrum of a 'discipline' is, of course, entirely appropriate.

*

The following is one version of the publicity and recruitment leaflet issued by the University of Kent. This dates from 1988, when over 700 applied for the twelve places available.

COMMUNICATIONS & IMAGE STUDIES

The role of communications and of images seems much more central in our society and culture than ever before. Almost overwhelmingly so.

We turn on the television, browse a newspaper, read a book, listen to a record, watch a film, play a video, send a letter, make a phone call, tune into the radio, put on a tape — all deeply familiar actions most of us take for granted.

YET THIS PARTICULAR combination of forms of communication is radically new in human history, even though each of those forms has developed from previous patterns of exchange and transmission of messages, information, and expression.

Likewise, images - of several different kinds - are an important part of our everyday life. Many of today's communications media involve considerable use of images, still and moving, printed and electronic. Other images abound in our culture: snapshots, postcards, paintings, posters, adverts, illustrations, maps. Visual imaging has a role in dreams and fantasies, in memories and expectations. In a wider sense, poets use 'images' and we all use our 'imagination'. We store images, glance at them, circulate them, buy and sell them, enjoy them. We seem almost unable to live without images of some kind.

Yet most of these forms of image and of image-making are not 'natural' but have had to be invented, many of them fairly recently.

However new our present pattern might be, every period and every culture has developed some form or forms of communication and some kind of image making.

Past Disciplines, Present Patterns

In the past, several disciplines have emerged in the continuing attempt to understand different aspects of communications (from voice to video) and of images (from art to ads), using a variety of methods and approaches (from sociology to semiotics). Most of these disciplines - from Art History to Film Studies, from Media Sociology to Linguistics - are already taught at Kent. But none of these seems able, by itself, to grasp the full range of the new developments that are taking place.

Just as there is now a re-shaping of, and new interactions between, 'communications' and 'images', so increasingly there is a need for the development of a new discipline, a new kind of inquiry, which can examine and explore these new interactions while placing them within a much longer and wider perspective than any already existing discipline can.

Obviously, this new discipline must build upon and develop from existing forms of study, just as the new situation has itself developed from the past. It will bring together the methods and achievements of, for example, art history and media studies, linguistics and philosophy, film and theatre studies. Only a university with a sufficiently flexible structure and a generously cooperative environment could hope to develop and offer such a field of study.

CIS: A new Degree

The new degree in 'Communications & Image Studies' - known as 'CIS' and unique to Kent - offers the opportunity to build upon existing disciplines and yet to develop an overview. No single student, however, could reasonably be expected to cover the entire field. Each will probably, in any case, have a preferred angle of interest.

The degree is therefore devised to offer you a structure (see below) in which you can emphasise one or other of the existing areas of study, but within the context of a deliberate interaction between the various elements in the degree and between the various other students, and teachers, who share an overall interest but have different particular specialisms.

For this reason, the degree is offered only as a full Honours programme. The course is arranged so that every CIS student will take 'core' courses concerned with both Communications and Images, but then have a wide range of options available from which to organise an individual package of interests. You might take most of your first year courses and your options from one field (in effect, making your degree a 'Combined Honours' programme) or you might include courses from a number of areas. You can also decide to replace an option course by your own individually constructed Project or Dissertation.

Core and Options

The core courses have developed through the cooperation of specialists in several areas, and are described below. The options are mainly courses already taught within the Humanities Faculty (by staff from Film, Drama, Art History, Philosophy, English etc.) with some further courses available from the Social Sciences Faculty (in Sociology, Anthropology, Politics), from Linguistics and from the Faculty of Information Technology (e.g. Computing courses). A selective list of these options is given later.

Teaching and Resources

Methods of teaching and of assessment and examination will match the flexibility and variety of the fields covered and courses chosen, but teaching on core courses will be mainly by small group discussion and workshops. CIS will have a number of specially equipped rooms for appropriate work on images and communications. The resources available to students will include the University's collection of 110,000 slides and a regularly updated 'teaching archive' of media material, as well as the usual audio-visual facilities. There is good liaison with, e.g., the Centre for the Study of Cartoons and Caricature and the Kent Institute for Art and Design; the considerable resources of both should be available for suitable project work.

The Degree Structure
The overall pattern of your degree would look like this:
PART I (First Year)
Three two-term courses chosen from existing Kent Humanities courses.
e.g., Historiography of Art; Post-War British Theatre in Performance, Computing for Humanities; Introduction to Film Narrative; Language and Society; Explorations in Reading; Fundamental Problems in Philosophy;
Plus one single-term interdisciplinary Topic, either CIS's own *Pop Porn Punk & Politics*, or, e.g. *The Gothic Imagination; Psychoanalysis & Language; Paris: Myth & Reality; Comedy; Science Fiction.*

PART II (Second and Third Years)
YEAR 2:
Communications & Culture: Problems & Approaches; Reading the Image & Option course
YEAR 3:
History & Theory of Imaging and *two* of the following:
Media, Culture & Society, Dissertation. or Project, Option course

The option courses normally available would include, e.g.
Film:
Film Theory; Early Film Form; British Cinema; Non-Narrative Cinema; Sexual Difference in the Cinema.

History & Theory of Art:
*Art Criticism; Mannerism, The Primitive; Abstraction &
Construction in the Twentieth Century; Art & Architecture of the
Renaissance; Patronages' Cultural Organisation.*

Drama:
*Radio Drama; Playwriting; Twentieth-Century British Theatre;
Women in Theatre; Comparative Dramaturgy.*

Literature/Language:
*Linguistics; Literature, Culture & Society; Explorations in English
Language; Rhetoric & History in the Classical World.*

Philosophy:
*Theory of Knowledge; Philosophy of Mind; Aesthetics;
Philosophy Of Psychoanalysis;Philosophy in Literature.*

Social Sciences:
*Political Communication Gf Mass Media;
Fascism; Social Communications.*

Computing:
Information Technology; Electronic Publishing.

Some of these option courses assume that you will have taken
the appropriate Part I course and some combinations of options
may be restricted by timetable requirements. The list of options
available will vary from year to year.

CORE COURSES

*COMMUNICATIONS & CULTURE: PROBLEMS AND
APPROACHES* This course (taught mainly by philosophers and
social anthropologists) will explore the field and conceptual
framework of the degree, bringing analytic and theoretical ideas
and terms (e.g. 'sign', 'rhetoric', 'post-structuralist') into critical
relation with real-life cases (e.g. page 3 of *The Sun,* popular
romance, cigarette ads). The aim will be to develop a
systematic, critical and workable framework of concepts through
studying a range of central 'texts', their contexts and conditions
of production and reception, and their relationships to a
changing wider culture. The initial theoretical focus will be on
attempts to analyse texts and images in primarily 'linguistic' and
'rhetorical' terms (e.g. do pictures *say* something? To whom?).

137

The examples and materials considered will be drawn primarily from popular culture, though the course is concerned to develop approaches appropriate to the understanding of cultural communication in general. In addition to participating in the lecture and seminar programme, students will prepare an extended essay on a theoretical issue of particular concern to them and also research a project of their own choice.

READING THE IMAGE This course (taught by art historians) aims to provide a systematic knowledge of the dominant tradition of visual representation in post-Renaissance Western art. Students are introduced to the theory and practice of perspective, both in the Renaissance and in relation to the repudiation of the traditional scheme in Cezanne and the Cubists. Various different ways of describing and interpreting the visual work of art are then discussed, concluding with a detailed study of photography, in its historical, aesthetic and social context.

HISTORY& THEORY OF IMAGING This course (which draws upon teachers in literature, philosophy, theology, computing and film) is divided into several units, each taught by a specialist. It examines philosophical notions of the image and the role of images in religious belief and practice; the relations between images and political power in different periods and societies; the functions of images in education and science; the growth of the 'image industries'. The course ranges from mediaeval images in Canterbury Cathedral to contemporary criticism of the 'simulation' society, from Byzantine iconoclasm to electronic image processing. Each unit and topic is placed within an overall historical inquiry which cumulatively provides the various material upon which a comprehensive theory of the cultural role of images can be based.

MEDIA, CULTURE AND SOCIETY The main focus of this course (taught by sociologists) is the mass media (television, radio, advertising, journalism, etc.) in the developed countries. It examines their political, cultural and historical backgrounds and traces the evolution of media institutions and audiences. Media technologies, professional organisations, systems of public regulation and markets for media products are each taken into account in explaining the social significance of contemporary communications. Media content (verbal, visual and textual) forms an important part of the course. The varieties of content are studied through generous use of cases and examples from TV, film and video, magazines, advertising, popular entertainment, in order to illustrate the range of techniques of analysis available and to introduce theories of media influence. The interaction between the modern media and trends in technology, social organisation and personal life-styles is discussed. Evidence of the convergence of the mass media with systems of cultural production based on telecommunications and computing is used as a basis for critical discussion of the 'information society' and related concepts.

Approaches & Prospects

Though the degree is based in Humanities you can approach CIS from several angles, including transfer from Social Sciences. Your own emphasis will be apparent in your particular combination or concentration of courses, and in any Project or Dissertation you undertake (which might develop from a core course or from an interest developed in an option course). Equally, you can think of CIS as helping you to prepare for future work in several existing areas of employment (arts administration, media researcher, advertising, journalism, television...). But the degree is not intended to provide technical training for particular jobs or even to produce general technologists of communications. Kent already has a Faculty of Information Technology with its own kind of degrees, although CIS can drawn upon their courses and resources. The emphasis of a degree situated primarily within Humanities and Social Sciences is critical and comprehensive rather than vocational.

Since new developments always take place within a wider history and a complex social context, and cannot easily be anticipated, CIS will be concerned with situating present patterns within much broader perspectives, both theoretical and historical. That combination of disciplines and perspectives is designed to enable you not only to understand what has already happened in this area but to have a wide basis from which to engage actively and flexibly in a rapidly changing future.

MARCH 1988

*

By 1994 the recruiting leaflet had changed, as had the degree programme, but several core components remained. This edited version omits simple repetitions from 1988 and highlights particularly the new courses which had developed and the questions applicants were asking by then. From the present persepective, the range, pedagogical approaches, and collaborative character of the degree seem barely conceivable. By 2000, of course, it had been shut down—just as the developments we had begun to explore in the 1980s were becoming pervasive.

COMMUNICATIONS & IMAGE STUDIES

You won't find many degree programmes with this particular title, so it's worth explaining why Kent has put together such a distinctive combination.

The degree was devised in the mid-1980s to anticipate changes that we could see coming for the mid-1990s and we're pleased that we seem to have got many of those changes right.

Today a lot of people are talking about the convergence of computers and television, of hypertext and multimedia, of the digital superhighway, of having 500 channels of TV or video on demand. A few years ago they were talking about cyberspace and the internet, or mirror worlds and virtual reality. Next year it might be another set of buzz words.

Whatever the current hype or fad, we do seem faced with a radically new convergence of communications technologies and with it new social, cultural, political and personal opportunities and possibilities.

At the same time, many people are puzzling over what seems an unexpected re-emergence of very old forms of behaviour and relationship, in newly assertive nationalisms and renewed conflicts of identity, old religious rivalries and energetic cultural revivalisms. In a few short years we have seen political boundaries and alliances, cultural traditions and self-definitions, transformed and reinvented.

In all this the role of images seems central: not simply the endless television images bringing us vivid news of turbulent events, or computer screens glowing with the latest graphic inventions, but more fundamentally the deep sense of new self-images and cultural identities being creatively or anxiously remade under the impact of both technological and political change.

Communications and Image Studies (known as CIS) was devised to explore these several contemporary developments, but not merely to see them as current novelties. Rather, we have attempted to situate these changes in a much longer historical perspective and a broader theoretical understanding, focusing on those two crucial terms: communications and image.

To do so we have brought together a unique combination of resources. CIS is not another media studies programme (though within the CIS programme you can take courses in media sociology taught by some of the best-known figures in the field); nor is it a film studies course (though since Kent was one of the first to establish such a programme you can certainly include film options); nor is it a computer science course (though Kent has one of the finest computing labs in the country and some of its courses are available to CIS students).

What CIS offers is the chance to bring together in your own thinking and your own practice precisely those convergences which are occurring in the larger world and which no single traditional discipline can hope to encompass by itself. CIS brings together literary critics and anthropologists, art historians and film theorists, media specialists and computer experts, philosophers and political analysts.

Obviously, though, we don't expect you suddenly to become expert in all these areas. The degree programme is devised so that you are given a wide range of individual choice but within a common framework shared with other CIS students. From the very first term we encourage CIS students to work together on practical projects (and to learn in the process the basic skills of video-editing, of photography, of computer graphics) while at the same time a seminar-based course prompts you to think for yourself about the intellectual tools and the information resources you will need to work within the overall shape of the degree. In that first year you also choose two other courses which reflect your own particular interests, whether film or art history, a new language or ancient history.

In the second year you have to take one core course, concerned with a number of critical issues in thinking about communications, and in your final year another core course looks at the history and theory of imaging, from cave art to Disneyland and beyond. Your other course each year can be chosen from a wide range and we expect CIS students to be adventurous in the combinations they choose. But the various interests represented in any one year tend to come together and constitute an overall perspective within which you make your own contribution. If by your final year you want to spend a lot of time working on your own specific practical project or extended dissertation you can do so, with a wealth of different expertise to draw upon - not least, by then, your fellow CIS students.

We've included later in this leaflet an overall outline of the degree and descriptions of some of the courses available to you, but bear in mind that CIS is still a growing and changing programme and we don't guarantee to remain with the same combinations every year!

Now, some *FAQ*. (Frequently Asked Questions)

How is the course examined?
(It's an interesting question why people are bothered by this question even before they start! Maybe it's the preoccupation with A levels?)

We examine courses within the degree in a variety of ways. All courses include an element of continuous coursework assessment (you write essays or produce videos or whatever, we mark them, those marks go towards your final grade for the course) but some courses have a traditional three-hour exam at the end, others have a 'take-away paper' (you get three days in which to do it), others don't have written exams but rely wholly on coursework. Some courses are practical so you produce a final video or computer presentation as your 'exam'; others allow you to write a long essay. In other words, we choose (and invite you to suggest) ways of assessing that are appropriate to each course. Your final degree result is worked out from the overall course grades you get in your second and third years.

How are courses taught? (Or: How do you learn?)

Most courses include some form of weekly lecture (though that may mean video screening or even multi-media presentations - we are a communications degree!) Some are practical skills courses. Some involve group workshops. Most have weekly seminars (discussion groups). And all involve you in doing a lot of private reading and thinking. You'll get experience of most of these ways of teaching and learning in your first year.

Can I spend a year abroad?

Yes, provided that you've chosen one of the overall CIS degree programmes that include a year abroad: either European Arts (CIS) or CIS in Europe. You can spend a year in, for example, Paris, Amsterdam, Lisbon, Bologna,

Munich (these may change) provided you already have or acquire during your first two years the appropriate language.

Is there any work experience included in the course?

Not as a formal part of the degree. A lot of CIS students do find their own work (preferably paid!) during the summer vacations (and we help them to find it) but we don't include any formal period of work experience within the term-time programme, partly because we're not primarily geared towards vocational training and partly because the programme is already busy enough! With two long summer vacations and several shorter ones it seems better to let you use that time rather than the actually rather short time you spend on campus.

If it's not vocational what sort of job can I get at the end of a CIS degree?

You will have done quite a lot of different things during your degree (history, art, film, computing, photography, video, even thinking!). And you will probably have been involved in some of the extra-curricular activities CIS students are drawn to: the film-making society, the campus radio station, the student newspaper. Any of these might lead you towards a particular area of work and some of the obvious ones are well trodden by CIS graduates already (the BBC, CNN, independent television companies, public relations, journalism, advertising). But we also try to encourage you to think about the new jobs and areas of work emerging with the new technologies (several CIS graduates are now designing and authoring CD-ROMS or working in multi-media) and to recognise that 'communications and images' covers a lot more than the mass media (for example, children's interactive games, tourism, museums). Since CIS is partly about the emerging new possibilities, don't just think in terms of the familiar old jobs.

But if it's not vocational (and it's not media studies or film studies or computing . .) what will I be doing all this time?

One answer is that you'll be getting an education. CIS is very firmly a humanities and social sciences degree. It isn't primarily about teaching you technical or practical skills (universities can rarely do that well—whatever they claim—especially in a field where the newest technology is always about a week old and very expensive!). You may well have thought as much about conflicts of ethnic identity in former Yugoslavia (the *Images of Identity* course is taught by someone with extensive field experience both there and in the Middle East) as about developments in postmodernist thought (one of us is writing a *Postmodernism for Beginners* book). You will have grappled with Plato (one of us has written a lot about Greek philosophy) as well as with media bias (another of us used to work with the Bad News Group), examined Byzantine iconoclasm (yes!) as well as how American television is already enshrined in TV museums (one of us wrote a thesis on that).

Can I combine CIS with another subject?

We only offer CIS as a single honours programme, but within the options available to you will be a number of courses taught by other Boards, such as History and Theory of Art, Sociology, Computing, Film Studies, Drama. The point of CIS is to bring these areas together in new ways, so we don't offer formal 50/50 combinations with other subjects, but by making your own selections carefully you can give your overall degree an emphasis in a particular area that interests you.

What resources does CIS have?

The main resource is, of course, the general facilities of the University, which includes a large library and lots of staff with different areas of expertise. The University also has, for example, a television studio, the Centre for me Study of Cartoons and Caricature, a large slide library (120,000 slides), and allows every student access to the global internet (world-wide electronic information network). More specifically, CIS has several rooms for its own equipment. We work with SVHS and VHS video editing decks, a variety of paint, graphics, titling and music computer programs, and photographic developing facilities. Once students have received basic instruction in this equipment the rooms are open to them 9 am to 10 pm and they can use the equipment as they wish. We update the equipment regularly, so any specific list would probably be out of date by the time you read this.

The overall pattern of your degree will look like this:

Two courses are specific to CIS and required of every CIS student:

Introduction to Image Skills
This is a hands-on workshop course which provides basic training in the video, photographic and computing facilities available to CIS students, including practical exercises and project work.

Introduction to CIS
This is a seminar based course which introduces modes of analysis and problems of method, focused mainly on contemporary popular culture.

You also take two more courses, chosen from the full range of Humanities Part I courses: e.g. Historiography of Art; Post-War British Theatre in Performance; Computing & Humanities; Introduction to Narrative Cinema; Self and Society; Fundamental Problems in Philosophy.

PART 11 (SECOND AND THIRD YEARS)

In each Part II year you take four courses: a compulsory core course and three other courses chosen from the range indicated below.

Year 2 core course: *Critical Issues in Culture & Communication*

Year 3 core course: *History & Theory of Imaging*

The three other courses each year are chosen from the following:
Reading the Image; The Photograph ; Media, Culture & Society; Modernity; Images of Identity; Other People/Other Places Everyday Images Representing Television; Image Technology (practical Course); Project or Dissertation (3rd Year only); an Option course (only one each year is allowed)
[The list of Options was largely that of 1988]

CORE COURSES

Critical Issues in Culture & Communication

This course examines the characteristics of human and animal communication practices, theories of visual and linguistic thinking, anthropological conceptions of world formation through language, notions of the sign in Saussure and Pierce, and of the 'unconscious of the sign' in Freud and Marx. These theories are explored in relation to advertising and the construction of desire, music and its 'meanings', cultural mythologies and subcultures, and the reformulation of images of community in Eastern and Western Europe after the collapse of the Soviet world order. The aim of the course is to familiarise students with a diverse and interdisciplinary range of concepts which are 'good to think with'.

The History & Theory of Imaging

This course involves specialist contributors from philosophy, theology, history and literature and covers such topics as: philosophical notions of the image and the role of images in religious belief and practice; the relations between images and political power in different periods and societies; the functions of images in education and science; the growth of the 'image industries.' The course ranges from mediaeval images in Canterbury Cathedral to contemporary criticism of the 'simulation' society, from Byzantine iconoclasm to the social significance of computerised image-making, placing each topic and issue within an overall historical inquiry which cumulatively provides the various material upon which a comprehensive theory of the cultural role of images might be based.

BASIC COURSES

Media, Culture & Society

This course focuses on the mass media (television, radio, advertising, journalism) in the developed countries. It examines their political, cultural and historical backgrounds and traces the evolution of media institutions and audiences. Media technologies, professional organisations, systems of public regulation and markets for media products are each taken into account in explaining the social significance of contemporary communications. The interaction between the modern media and trends in technology, social organisation and personal life-styles is discussed. Evidence of the convergence of the mass media with systems of cultural production based on tele-communications and computing is used as a basis for critical discussion of the 'information society' and related concepts.

Images of Identity: Self/Community/Nation

This course looks at the way the self is constituted within various webs of communications and interaction, including the tensions involved in that constitution. Images and practices from various stages of life in different cultures are examined to illuminate the way desires are shaped and people assume, and refuse, particular identities and self-images. Psychoanalytic concepts are developed to understand the process of gender positioning, and the social functions of antagonism and warfare are explored in relation to such issues as deviance, anti-colonialism, resurgent fundamentalisms and ethnicities.

Modernity

The term 'Modernity' implies a particular kind of consciousness and attitude, often with ambiguous connotations: 'progress', but also transience, rootlessness. The course explores the sources of this ambivalence, through analysing the history and structure of the experience of modernity as it has developed in Western societies. It examines the shaping and control of body experiences through the 'civilisation' of behaviour, the experience of urban life, and the influence of fashion, consumerism, and the fantasy structure of literature and the media in shaping gender, identity, and aspirations. The course also explores what is excluded or devalued by 'modernity': the carnivalesque, the 'primitive', madness, nature, the supernatural, aspects of the feminine -these suppressed and tabooed meanings and dimensions which continue to fascinate and act as a source of transgression and conflict.

Everyday Images

This course examines contemporary visual messages which tend to be overlooked because they seem transparent, anonymous, unaesthetic or merely superficial, those daily encounters with images on hoardings, packets, exhibition spaces, as well as in newspapers, comics, surrealistic adverts and museum displays. The course interrogates our perceptions of 'everydayness' in the light of close readings informed by semiotics and various models of communication.

Other People, Other Places

This course considers the various ways imagining the other and imaging the self have combined in the historically specific practices and representations of exploration, colonisation, travel and tourism. The course surveys the development of Western concepts of travel, from Herodotus to mediaeval pilgrimage, from Columbus to the

Grand Tour, from colonial expansion to contemporary ethnographic museums, from Disneyland to the heritage industry.

Reading the Image

This course aims to provide a systematic knowledge of the dominant tradition of visual representations in post-Renaissance Western art. Students are introduced to the theory and practice of perspective, both in the Renaissance and in relation to the repudiation of the traditional scheme in Cezanne and the Cubists. Various ways of describing and interpreting the visual work of art are then discussed, concluding with a detailed study of photography, in its historical, aesthetic and social context.

The Photograph: Culture, History, Aesthetic

Photography is now recognised as a major medium of visual communication and one of the most obvious forms through which we construct an image of the modern world. Yet despite its familiarity, its status and meaning remain ambiguous and problematic. By looking at the photograph in a series of historical, cultural and aesthetic contexts, the course investigates the specific 'language' of the photograph and how it contributes to our image of the world.

Image Technology

This course offers hands-on exploration of multi-media presentation possibilities, drawing upon video and computer facilities, including hypertext, morphing, chromakey, digital image manipulation and composition. Each student devises and develops a specific application or project utilising the facilities available and the course includes a critical overview of current developments in the multi-media field.

*

TEACHING, MULTIMEDIA, AND THE INTERNET

When I said to friends, back in England, that I was coming to India to talk about the relation between teaching and multimedia, there tended to be a predictable reaction of surprise: multimedia in India? After all, the dominant images of India, still, in England are likely to be ones of urban deprivation or idyllic rural scenes, and not of advanced computers. I had then to remind such friends that India is also the country with the second highest number of professional computer programmers, about 180,000, with software exports last year [1994] worth some 2.4 crore rupees, from an industry that now employs 1.4 lakh personnel.

Yet after I had arrived in India and found myself, for example, up in the Khasi hills just beyond Shillong, seeing for myself those tiny clusters of huts perched at the very edge of precipitous ravines, with the children of those families living in such apparent remoteness from anything to do with computers, I again had to remind myself why talking about advanced multimedia systems might nevertheless be a contribution to pondering the future of humanities in India, as elsewhere. After all, those children live by a major arterial road, which daily carries coal down to Guwahati and exports out to Bangladesh, and also carries those children on school buses to Shillong. And Shillong, as this very conference indicates, can easily be an avenue out to a global communication system. My own arrangements for coming to the conference were largely conducted through an e-mail link via Hyderabad. Just three years ago even getting a fax from Canterbury to Hyderabad was difficult. Things can change, quickly.

Moreover, India now has, by some criteria, the largest educated middle class of any nation, some 100 million people, a massive presence even within a population larger than Africa and Latin America combined. And clearly some at least of that enormous number have indeed become involved in multimedia and associated developments like the internet—just a casual reading of the Indian press today alerts me to a major conference on multimedia in Bombay, to the fact that one service provider is extending its internet access facility to Ahmedabad, Baroda, Delhi, Calcutta, Madras, that a college of commerce has recently offered internet and multimedia courses and attracted so many extra students that it had to open a new computer laboratory, that a cybercafe offering public internet access has now opened in Bombay. Things are changing, quickly.

But one could still ask what does all this have to do with the future of teaching Humanities? Aren't computers still basically a matter for computer scientists, or at best businessmen and administrators? It's worth then starting from the point that there simply will be no future for what we think of as the Humanities, with its traditional emphasis on the capacity to read and write, unless our children continue to learn to read and write—which includes that familiar childhood horror: learning to spell. Allow me to take my initial evidence from my own context. My seven-year-old son is a good example of the problems of maintaining continuity of the most basic elements of culture across the new generation gaps. Familiar almost since infancy with television, video, radio, records, audio tapes, what space is there for reading, what incentive for him to master that most intimate and intricate of deep-seated skills? In particular, how is he to tackle the amazing complexities of English spelling, which is barely coherent even to the most practised among us? We can, of course, continue to impose and insist, in the traditional ways, by rote learning and intensive practice. But the attractions of television and the allurement of the screen will intrude and distract. In that world of visual and aural pleasures how can a child even begin to learn to spell? Here then, as a starting point, is one area where the multimedia computer may indicate some of its educational potential.

So let us consider a new form of spelling lesson, a multimedia CD-ROM entitled *Arthur's Teacher Trouble*. When my seven year old starts the program a screen appears with an image of an open book with the words 'Living Books' inside it, and the words are bouncing up and down to a catchy tune. The image of the book on the screen fades into that of a lively cartoon figure who speaks in a welcoming and cheerful voice, introducing the program as a story that the child can either have read to him or her or play directly. While the child makes up its mind which button to click on, to choose between these options, the friendly rabbit-like figure goes into a dance sufficiently amusing that most children will deliberately wait a while before clicking on either the 'read' or 'play' button. Once they decide to play, for example, the figure gives a cheery "Bye" and the screen fades into the first frame or page of the story.

Text now appears across the top portion of a colourful picture of a school corridor and as a voice reads the text the picture is animated by a troop of cartoon animal-like children coming into the corridor from their classroom, together with a teacher who is clearly something of a disciplinarian, as well as looking like a goofy rat. The children include a mouse-like figure we come to know as Arthur. As the text finishes being read, a cursor appears on the screen so that the child can now move the mouse (the computer device, not Arthur!) and click on various parts of the picture to make all sorts of things happen. The noticeboard in the corridor is full of posters to make familiar school activities: clicking on the choir notice activates a school choir that ends in a caterwauling howl, clicking on the sports notice animates a figure wielding a baseball-bat who crashes a ball through an off-screen window, clicking on the botany notice lets loose a lively insect that runs around the screen, including down the neck of the teacher, and clicking on the teacher himself results in some surprising changes of clothes for him: one quick-change effect leaves the sober man dressed as Elvis Presley.

A child probably takes about ten minutes to explore this first page's hidden surprises before they click on an arrow to turn to the next page-screen, where again a voice reads the text while each word of the text highlights in turn. The child may by now have realized that as well as the pictorial elements on each page they can also click on any word and activate the corresponding sounds. A child in the early days of reading will be held by this immediate connection between sounds, highlighted word and story.

Each further page (there are 24) has its levels of interactive surprises, but what begins to emerge as the overall story-line is that the teacher has entered the class in a spelling competition, a Spellathon, and our hero, Arthur, is selected as one of the leading contenders. In watching this story unfold the child is also drawn into several spelling exercises. As Arthur tries to learn a list of words, those words are shown on screen and can be activated by the child playing the program. Clicking on a word not only prompts a voice to spell out the letters but also initiates some associated action: clicking on 'Banana' results in a monkey spraying bananas across the screen, 'Vacuum' prompt a vacuum cleaner to suck up half the page and spew it out, the 'Whale' word disappears beneath waves and upsets the 'Submarine' word, and so on.

It would take too long to describe in detail this or any of the other similar CD-ROM 'edutainment' products now available. But the essential point is that children *enjoy* these inter-active story-books. Built into them are layers of immediate micro-rewards, an amusing action or tune or image that appears when the child activates some element that is at the same time an instructional element. The incentive to learn, to master the spelling routine or whatever, is immediately reinforced by a local bonus. The story as a whole also carries the further and familiar pleasures of overall narrative and eventual closure, while also allowing the child freedom to move through the pages in an order of personal preference. Once a child has been through this program he tends to leap next time to favourite pages and these surprisingly often include those very spelling lessons which in another mode they might well turn away from and avoid. To make spelling enjoyable is a major pedagogical achievement! It's also worth noting that at the heart of this apparently up-to-the-minute educational program are some very traditional conceptions of education. The spelling test is still a matter of memory and of learning practice, the roles of teacher and pupil are clearly formalized and old-fashioned, classroom activities are competitively structured. Arguably, this aspect of the program indicates reluctance, in this example, to take further the opportunities afforded by education multi-media for re-thinking some of our received assumptions, even while the effect of the program itself modifies some of them in practice.

But why choose this example to highlight: a children's tale, a basic skill lesson? What has this to do with the future of humanities teaching at university level? Let me emphasize one aspect of that program. The child is learning to control an action, which someone else undertakes: the teacher speaks when the child clicks on him, the rabbit dances, the voice speaks. These are, at one level, substitutes for the child's own activities and speech, but at another level the child is learning to make such things happen on its own behalf, is taking them over and making them its own. What is involved here is a variation on that essential process which is constitutive of all education: the process of quotation. All children learn by mimicking, by imitating, by quoting others' words and actions. We all as children take over phrases, tones, intonations, from parents and others. Only through that mimicking entry into the language of our tribe can we eventually arrive at our own speech, find our own words to say. But always our words are received and heard from others in the first place. We are most intimately shaped by what we repeat from others.

This remains true at the most sophisticated level also. So much academic writing is a form of quotation, of paraphrase, of re-cycling. To take one example: an academic article on 'Culture and Cultural Planning in India' (I leave the author anonymous since my comments might be taken too simply as criticism) comprises 19 printed pages, of which 11 pages paraphrase other writers, with footnoted references to the texts being summarized, while a further five pages consist of *verbatim* lengthy quotations from other writers—so some 16 pages out of 19 could be regarded as quotation. This is what academics, notoriously, do. But to be able to do so is precisely what it means to enter the chain of texts that constitute a field, a discipline. Quotation is the matter of education.

Along with what I will call mapping: we also have to learn, whether as children, postgraduates or professors, to order and organize our quotations, to orient our listeners or readers in a clear direction, just as we need to know our own way around a field or form of discourse. We need to be confident about which quotations to select, how the various excerpts, citations, references, examples, are to be related to each other. A merely random mimicking and repetition of others' words or ideas is neither a good exam answer nor an adequate professional contribution. We need our own mental map of the intellectual territory in order to guide others. And eventually we learn to make new maps, new territories.

Now think about these two most basic aspects of education in terms of the new multimedia technologies available. I am writing this piece using a word processor and by now most academics will be familiar with such programs. They allow us to cut and paste words or blocks of text, to revise our clumsy expressions endlessly, without the old labour of re-typing whole pages or even entire papers each time. What such word-processing programs allow and even encourage is yet more quotation, because I can cut and paste not only my own provisional words, as I move paragraphs or sentences around within my document, but also the words of others which I am deploying in my text. Until recently, I still had to type such extracts or quotations into my document in the first place: a considerable discouragement to lengthy excerpts. Now, I can make my quotations work for me at a click of the mouse, they are my avatars and agents, I can get to act on my behalf and under my direction —like the child activating cartoon figures in *Arthur's Teacher Trouble*.

If the text I want to incorporate is already in electronic form, on a floppy disk for example, I can much more easily cut and paste a passage from it. The world of professional humanities productivity begins to change even with that simple possibility, and issues of digital plagiarism rapidly loom. But what if I don't just have the electronic text of some friend's article sent to me on a floppy, but I have, for example, the entire corpus of Shakespeare on my hard disk and I can cut and paste quotations from any play into my piece with immediate ease—particularly if I can also search the full text of Shakespeare electronically and instantly. Compiling articles based on Shakespeare's use of imagery, for example, becomes dangerously easy. Take a further step: I can now have the whole of the *Encyclopaedia Britannica* on a CD-ROM next to my computer, together with the *Oxford English Dictionary* on another CD-ROM. I can therefore cut and paste from several million words of authoritative text, together with thousands of quotations already embedded in the *OED*. If I can afford it, I can already have almost the entire canonical corpus of English poetry and drama on a couple of CD-ROMs and perhaps in a few years time I will be able to have the entire Library of Congress on a set of mega-CD-ROMs on my desk. What happens to the process, including the authority and prestige, of scholarly quotation when it no longer involves going to the library, searching through shelves, transcribing from sources, but the equivalent of all this can be done from a desktop in a few minutes of digital search and retrieval? Perhaps personal mapping becomes even more important.

But this is only the beginning. My word processor allows me to cut and paste sound and images too. If I have not just the text of a Shakespeare play but also an audio or video tape of it, I can include in my document a spoken quotation or even an extract from a video of the play I am writing about. I can also record my own spoken rendition of a poem I want to analyze and include that as an embedded 'object' inside my text. I can then send that combination of sound and text or even video to a colleague on disk or—and this is a further step—across the Internet. Imagine what this does to student essays. I can set an assignment on *The Waste Land* and expect my students not only to write about the poem, with quotations from Eliot's text, but also to quote Eliot's voice actually reading that text, together with their own alternative spoken version if they so wish. I can mark their essays with Eliot's voice in my own ears whenever appropriate.

Yet this is now pretty amateur stuff, for it is not just the academic or the student essay-writer who can compose such multi-media versions of a play or a poem. Let me describe a second example of a multimedia program, this time aimed at somewhat older children than *Arthur's Teacher Trouble*. My teenage daughter is studying *Romeo and Juliet* in school this term. The class will of course read the text, they will act out scenes, and they will probably go to a theatre performance, and perhaps watch a video of the television production from a few years ago. But what is now also possible is that each student can work with a CD-ROM of *Romeo and Juliet* published by the BBC in conjunction with Harper Collins and Attica. And that CD-ROM deploys essentially a set of variations on the processes we have already seen in *Arthur's Teacher Trouble*.

Again there is text, the entire play scrollable down the left side of the screen, with a spoken version audible by clicking on a button. On the right of the screen is a kind of playing area, displaying a picture of each character currently 'on stage' in the text. Across the bottom of the screen is a bank of buttons allowing access to a variety of written, oral and visual material concerning Shakespeare's life and times, his theatre, aspects of each character, spoken examples of different forms of verse in the play, etc. When a student clicks on a word in the play-text an explanation may pop up, or a gloss on its Elizabethan usage. Scenes from the play may be viewed in a video window on screen, or the student may choose simply to hear a scene acted while following the written text on screen or in a printed edition. As with *Arthur's Teacher Trouble* there is throughout an element of instant feedback and micro-reward: when a student clicks on a picture of the Globe theatre, for example, a larger or more detailed picture might appear or a video begins playing or a snatch of Elizabethan music might play.

These interactive and exploratory elements may indeed stimulate and sustain a certain kind of interest but, as with *Arthur's Teacher Trouble,* there are some problematic aspects. Having a plethora of options and forms of information accessible at a click or two may militate against a concentrated and sustained attention to the play. It may also encourage a certain laziness of response: if the program doesn't provide a gloss, the student doesn't seek further. Or students may not critically assess the explanatory or critical comments built into the presentation. Crucially perhaps, the CD-ROM still treats the play primarily as a text with visual *illustrations*, rather than as a performance scored *from* a text, and the potential for interactive exploration of alternative solutions to staging scenes, for example, is not developed. But of course the CD-ROM should not stand alone, without a student having access to other versions, productions, and critical comments. The familiar accusation that such multimedia programs are no substitute for books is understandable, but a book is in any case no substitute for a play, and there is no reason why books and CD-ROMs, theatre visits and class performances, cannot all be combined in an overall pedagogic strategy.

Now take a few more steps. Educational multi-media presentations (and what could be more multi-media than Shakespeare's's own theatrical practice?) need not be confined to a local resource like CD-ROM. If my computer is linked into the world wide web I can now download the entire corpus of Shakespeare's play from the 'Shakespeare Home Page' to be found at [http://the-tech.mit.edu /Shakespeare/other/html], or if I am working on Jane Austen I can access not only complete hypertext versions of all Austen's novels but also documentation, commentary, maps, letters, critical essays, all from the 'Jane Austen Home Page' at [http://uts.cc.utexas.edu/-chruch/janeinfo.html]. Most major authors now have similar home pages or web-sites, maintained by academic departments or enthusiasts.

With the capacity digitally to transmit texts and images, sound and moving pictures, the web is now becoming a world-wide resource bank on almost every conceivable topic, including those central to humanities. For example, in teaching art history I can not only have on my desk CD-ROMs with the complete catalogue of paintings in the London National Gallery or generous selections of paintings from the Louvre, the Uffizi, or the Frick Gallery in New York, but increasingly I can also access and download on-line art galleries. When the Tate Gallery in London recently staged a major Cezanne exhibition, Corbis simultaneously released a CD-ROM of Cezanne's paintings while at the same time the WebMusuem based in Paris made freely available some 100 digital versions of Cezanne paintings on the Internet, together with considerable documentation. A recent *Electronic Guide* to art history lists some 300 CD-ROMs, websites and other electronic resources available in that field alone.

In accessing and using all these resources I am still in effect operating a cut and paste, or quotation, process on material which may be on my hard disk, a CD-ROM in my own computer, or some massive data archive half-way across the world. But this process of quoting from a widespread range of sources increasingly passes directly into that other crucial educational process, that of mapping, of orienting oneself in a field of knowledge. In the past, much of scholarship consisted of physically browsing through library holdings, periodicals, books, and archives, while constructing a mental map of a specific intellectual field. But now the physical exploration is increasingly reshaped as electronic navigation through quite new configurations of knowledge organization. I now have to know my way around a changing landscape ofweb-sites and resource lists while not being swept away by a sense of information overload. When asked recently for reading suggestions on North American Indian culture I browsed the internet and within minutes found a site-list of several hundred addresses, each of them populated with personal home pages, archives, image galleries, collections of documents. How to establish one's critical bearings in this new electronic territory is a skill we will increasingly have to learn and teach: not only how to find appropriate sites but how to assess them, what protocols of credibility and reliability to work from, what ethics of acknowledgement, what principles of reference. These may be new variations on old problems, but the overall picture is also one of quite unprecedented opportunities. New maps and new kinds of maps are possible.

Moreover, the very mechanism by which I access all this material is the same mechanism that allows me to contribute to it. Insofar as the essential process is one of cutting and pasting, of quotation and digital reproduction, I am in any case incorporating this material into a document or composition of my own, which can then be re-disseminated onto the net. The most exciting aspect of being involved in multimedia is not the use of already finished products for teaching, such as *Romeo and Juliet*, but the opportunity it gives students to compose their own multimedia products. At its simplest, to produce the multimedia essay on Eliot suggested earlier but also more elaborate and productive exercises, a multimedia version of *The Waste Land* itself, or a virtual gallery of an artist's work, as in one of my students' digital reconstructions of de Chirico's paintings as an inter-connected labyrinthine city. Not just composition either but publication and distribution. A web site or home page is accessible by the whole Internet population without the traditional publishing costs of physical distribution. A student with a home page can have his or her essay read by 20 million net browsers.

By now, the potential of these technologies and resources for changes in humanities teaching should be sufficiently clear. It is time to step back and reconsider the overall picture. The emergence of the computer, and in particular the globally interlinked computer network known as the web or the internet, can be regarded as the most recent stage in a quest at the heart of a certain tradition within humanities: the drive to find means to disseminate what we now call culture.

There is a specifically English version of this quest from the time of Coleridge onwards. Coleridge envisaged a kind of intelligentsia as a variant of the ecclesiastical clergy, what he called the 'clerisy', each acting as a local repository of what Matthew Arnold was to call 'the best that has been thought and written'. Arnold's own version of the clerisy was the 'aliens' : figures somehow dissociated from any specific class allegiance and dedicated to making available 'sweetness and light'. For Arnold, the distribution mechanism was to be primarily the printed periodical which could reach into every household, though Arnold as a schools inspector also held out some hope for the educational institutions. For John Henry Newman, the dissemination of 'culture' was much more firmly associated both with the older model of the clergy and with the idea of the university. F. R. Leavis inherited all these emphases, in his long effort both to make university English departments the critical centre of culture and to disseminate his positions through the journal form, in *Scrutiny*.

Such notions of the critic as agent of culture still lie behind much of the ideology of the humanities. But the dominant dissemination mechanism for some time has been television, film, video, radio, and the audio-visual rather than print-based forms of mass communication. What is then interesting about the emergence of the computer is that a similar ambition, albeit in a commercial mode, is clearly at work. Bill Gates's proclaimed wish to have a computer in every home, or the drive of internet providers to expand the on-line population to the entire globe, are a reprise of the Coleridgean ambition to have the clerisy present in every locality or Arnold's belief in the capacity of periodicals to enter every household. Of course, crucial differences are apparent. The material to be found on the net is not predominantly what Arnold would have recognized as issuing forth sweetness and light and, increasingly, commercially oriented services and products are populating the net. Yet the potential remains: when I can download whole archives of Tibetan music, or galleries of aboriginal art, or masses of documentation on native American cultural practices, there is a genuine sense in which the basis for a shared global culture is being formed on my and every other desktop.

If we now return to India, the specificities of the Indian cultural situation might be emphasized. The relationships between print, audio-visual and electronic modes of communication, their cultural weight and significance, may well take very various forms across different national or geographical spaces. The several functions of the oral in India, the complex relations between ancient traditions of instruction and new forms of interactivity, above all perhaps the diversity of languages and scripts (though here distributed digital sound offers real possibilities), even the specific influence of the Indian film industry upon visual sensibilities, the class, gender and geographical aspects of access to computers—all such factors make highly problematic any attempt merely to map onto the Indian situation the exciting new developments of multimedia elsewhere. Similarly, the political and economic contexts for debates and decisions about national and global information super-highways can be very various indeed. How telecommunications policy might include widespread access to these new services and opportunities is a pressing issue in every country and is clearly taking specific forms in India, where, for example, the potential role of wireless communication and satellite transmissions may be more salient than elsewhere.

Yet if we are to think about 'what is needed now' in India and in the humanities, it may be that an India already well advanced in the technical and software aspects of the new information technologies is in a position to embark upon a quite exemplary experiment in national educational networking. Providing Internet and World Wide Web facilities throughout at least the university sector may involve considerable investment but potential benefits would include not just individual academic access to global on-line research resources, including full-text journals and publications otherwise expensive for libraries to obtain, but also the transformation of inter-university communication and cooperation within India. At the simplest administrative level, the Internet can provide electronic substitutes for letters, memos, faxes, the distribution of papers, reports, and files, both within a campus and between sites. A university website accessible to its own students can not only replace the local provision and distribution of printed notices, course information, reading lists, teaching materials, but also provide opportunities for pooling teaching resources between universities. Even the major cost of revision and updating of printed course material dissolves in their electronic equivalents. A policy of commissioning copyright-free innovative teaching materials (including multimedia) for national electronic distribution would be worth pursuing. Joint research projects involving distant departments become more feasible, while publication of staff papers on a local web site is effectively carried through to worldwide dissemination.

Much of this is becoming rapidly familiar and presumably government ministries are already assessing the potential and difficulties of such investment in electronic infrastructure. But these developments also require forceful support from within communities which might benefit from them and established humanities academics perhaps need further persuading—while a new generation of bright Indian postgraduates are in danger of spending time abroad with easy access to such facilities only to find themselves electronically disenfranchised on return.

The details of how one might begin to implement such a program are obviously for other occasions, but in concluding it might be worth hoping that, some day, an electronic network linking every school in India might mean that those children up in the Khasi hills will also be only a click away from the rest of the global community.

(Note : The figures presented in the beginning of the essay had certainly increased by 2002, when this paper was finally published in India. The paper was actually written in 1995 and presented at the CIEFL Shillong International Seminar on 'Teaching of Humanities: What is Needed Now?'. The spoken paper was accompanied by video demonstrations of the programs and software discussed, since no computer was then available in Shillong even for demonstration purposes. The paper deliberately retains an oral delivery mode and is simply one version of several delivered in various settings across India in the early 1990s. I leave it otherwise unrevised as a record of how much was to change —and yet remain the same.)

To be continued

* * *

www.ingramcontent.com/pod-product-compliance
Lightning Source LLC
Chambersburg PA
CBHW071458070426
42452CB00041B/1925